G1 £10-00

G1 £10-00

~Classic~ OCEAN LINERS

Patrick Stephens Limited, part of Thorsons, a division of the Collins Publishing Group, has published authoritative, quality books for enthusiasts for more than twenty years. During that time the company has established a reputation as one of the world's leading publishers of books on aviation, maritime, military, model-making, motor cycling, motoring, motor racing, railway and railway modelling subjects. Readers or authors with suggestions for books they would like to see published are invited to write to: The Editorial Director, Patrick Stephens Limited, Thorsons Publishing Group, Wellingborough, Northants, NN8 2RQ.

Classic
OCEAN LINERS

FRANK · O · BRAYNARD

Volume 1
BERENGARIA
LEVIATHAN
& MAJESTIC

PSL

Patrick Stephens Limited

First published in 1990

British Library Cataloguing in Publication Data
Braynard, Frank O. (Frank Osborn), *1916-*
Classic ocean liners.
Vol. 1: Berengaria, Leviathan and Majestic
I. Title
387.2'432

ISBN 1-85260-151-5

Front endpaper Whistles sounding, *Imperator*, later to become *Berengaria*, on her trials in the River Elbe in 1913.

Rear endpaper Farewell to *Leviathan*, on her way to the scrapyard in 1938.

Patrick Stephens Limited is part of the Thorsons Publishing Group, Wellingborough, Northamptonshire NN8 2RQ, England.

Typeset by MJL Limited, Hitchin, Herts
Printed and bound in Great Britain by
Butler & Tanner Ltd, Frome and London

1 3 5 7 9 10 8 6 4 2

CONTENTS

INTRODUCTION

This is the first of a new series of liner books designed to tell in some depth the lives of great liners of the past, three or four at a time. First, let me mention what I propose to cover in the next volume, as I would welcome any personal memories, photos or artefacts to do with these 'classic liners'. The next volume will feature the *Rex* and the *Conte di Savoia*. After that I hope to do a volume on the *Bremen* and the *Europa*, and then a volume on the *Mauretania, Lusitania* and *Aquitania*. Now back to Classic Liners Vol 1 and a few words about Albert Ballin.

Albert Ballin, the German genius who made Hamburg American Line the world's largest shipping company, was born on August 15, 1857, in Hamburg. This book is about the three superships that he ordered shortly before the first World War, *Imperator, Vaterland* and *Bismarck*, which were the first liners to exceed 50,000 tons. Their story, with over 200 photographs, is the meat of this volume.

The youngest of ten, in his youth Ballin was beset with many maladies. Music was his favourite subject, and from his earliest days he displayed a passion for books. He had a phenomenal memory and was quickly recognized as a gifted lad. In 1874 at the age of 17 he was projected into the world of men. The death of his father, and the disinterest of his elder brothers, gave him full responsibility in a small emigration agency called Morris & Co.

Albert Ballin, the genius who planned a weekly express service from Hamburg to New York maintained by 50,000-ton liners. He led the efforts in Germany to prevent the First World War.

This firm routed emigrants from Germany to America via Liverpool. It used the Keystone Line, an American company that had built four small steamers to run between Liverpool and Philadelphia. From the beginning, young Ballin cultivated the British representatives of this line. He learned to speak English well and made many trips to Great Britain. Ballin was quickly recognized as a man to be respected, and in the first six years of his management the number of emigrants from Hamburg rose from 25,000 to 123,000.

In his first major move he decided that routing emigrants via England was not the best way to serve the hordes of people eager to get to the New World, and he decided to turn two small German freighters into emigrant ships. In his first year he carried 4,000 emigrants. In the next, the total was 11,000. By 1883 he was moving more than a quarter as many as Hamburg Amerikanische, the Hamburg American Line. His success was extraordinary. By 1885 he was operating under a favourable agreement with Hapag, as Hamburg American was called for short.

At this time Hapag was suffering from tired management. Their arch rival, the younger North German Lloyd, had moved out in front. Ballin watched. Then, the next year, Hapag made one of the most astute moves in its long history—they hired Ballin and made him head of their premier North Atlantic passenger division. As one biographer wrote: 'He proved his worth almost at once, and within a few years became one of the greatest personalities ever known in the long history of North Atlantic and, indeed, world shipping.' The year was 1886. Ballin had arrived.

Although only 29, Ballin was already accustomed to move in a decisive and dramatic fashion. One of his first steps was to visit New York and name a new representative for Hapag in America. He chose the noted ex-German liberal Carl Schurz. Reactionary forces had defeated Schurz in 1848, when he had tried to create a liberal democracy in Prussia, and he had been forced to flee to America. By 1886 he had become one of the best-known political figures in the United States. Ballin could not have made a better choice.

Within two years the brilliant young Jew was virtually running Hapag. In 1897, 11 years later, he became managing director. The scene was set for his two greatest adventures—his efforts to stop the impending war between England and Germany, and his decision to build the three largest ships in the world.

In very simplified terms, there were two major currents in pre-first World War Germany. One is typified by Ballin, the self-made genius, cosmopolitan, peace-loving, but through-and-through German, who drove himself from obscurity to a position of leadership in world shipping. The other, personified by Bismarck, the war-loving, aristocratic, anti-Semitic statesman whose energy had helped to create a new state out of a disjointed collection of kingdoms and principalities. Attempting to lead the newly-united Germany, with one foot in each camp, was Kaiser Wilhelm II, a jovial, weak, partly crippled cousin of Britain's King George V. Had the 'Ballin' faction won, what a different world we would have today.

This is how things were, using the broad brush approach, shortly after the turn of the century, when Ballin began to consider the idea of a weekly service from Hamburg to New York, one liner sailing each week. They would have to be large, and they would have to be fast, perhaps contenders for the Blue Riband. The stage was set for instituting the largest new liner construction programme ever. At the same time there came into focus the old Prussian anti-Semitism, led by the Kaiser's wife, Auguste Victoria, and Admiral von Tirpitz. One major goal of these zealots was to break the ties that Ballin had established with the Kaiser. These bonds were so strong that Ballin's home in Hamburg had come to be known as the 'little Potsdam', because the Kaiser visited there so often (Potsdam being the name of the Kaiser's castle). Ballin had cultivated the Kaiser's friendship by such means as providing great liners as floating hotels for his use during German naval reviews off Kiel, and by a programme of building larger and more luxurious passenger ships he had stimulated the Kaiser's love of the sea. An example of the Kaiser's pride in his merchant marine can be seen in his instructions to the builders of a subway in Hamburg. It would become an 'elevated train' when it looped itself close to the waterfront, so that 'our citizens can see the great ships taking the German flag to all parts of the world,' the German Emperor pontificated—and so the subway remains to this day.

One of the Ballin's most ardent admirers in Great Britain was Sir Ernest Cassel, prominent banker. Through him Ballin had developed close ties with England's Edward VII, and he watched with alarm the growing naval and colonial rivalries between England and Germany. Ballin worked for years to counter these serious causes of hostility; his efforts are reviewed in the first volume of my *Leviathan* six-volume series on the *Vaterland/Leviathan*.

Opposing all of Ballin's work toward peace was Auguste Victoria. Ballin had named two ships after her to get into her good graces, but to no avail. Besides being anti-Semitic, she looked upon Ballin as an example of the newly-rich merchant class which she hated. Her natural ally was Admiral von Tirpitz. At first it seemed that with his first and second 50,000 ton superships, Ballin was winning the battle for the Kaiser's support. But then the Kaiserin triumphed, cutting Ballin out of the Emperor's circle and permitting the war drums to roll uncontested.

Symbolizing the might of the Kaiser's Germany, a model of the stem of Imperator, *with its remarkable eagle figurehead. This picture appeared in the* New York Tribune *in 1913.*

Frank O. Braynard
Sea Cliff, New York

1

BERENGARIA

〰〰〰〰〰〰

*T*he world's first ocean liner of over 50,000 gross tons was the German *Imperator*, to be known through most of her life as the famous *Berengaria*, of Cunard Line. We begin our account of Hamburg-American Line's 'Big Three' with the story of this ship.

The first of the 'Big Three' was designated Hull Number 314 when she was laid down in Hamburg in 1910. Ballin's biographer, Bernhard Huldermann, credited the famous Hapag leader with a major share of the actual design of the new trio. He wrote:

The big passenger boats of the Hapag have been described as the outcome of Ballin's imaginative brain. This they were indeed, and in many instances it is scarcely possible to say how far the credit for building them is due to the naval architect and how far it is due to Ballin.

Rarely had there been a shipowner who was so close to the actual design of his new steamers as Ballin. Rarely, indeed, probably never before on such a mammoth scale. But in fact there had never been a Ballin before. He was unique.

As the three-ship dream evolved, Ballin had

American artist, Bishop, did this fine bow view. This is his version done before the figurehead was added. In due course he repainted the bow to include it.

made two decisions: he would call the first of the great trio the *Europa*, and she would be built in Germany, with the second being constructed in Belfast. He commissioned the well-known American marine artist Fred Pansing to paint his new *Europa*. Pansing did two most appealing paintings for Ballin. One was a broadside. It showed the new ship going from left to right, with masses of smoke coming from all three funnels and the Hapag house flag blowing forward at the very stem. Both upper and lower enclosed promenades were conventional promenade decks. Nine lifeboats were on the boat deck on either side. The white paint extended down over the first hull deck, called E Deck on the ship's plans. There was no visible decoration at the stem. The second Pansing work was a bow-on view.

In June, 1910, roughly three years after serious design work had been begun, the keel of the first of Ballin's Big Three was laid, at the Hamburg yards of the A. G. Vulcan Works. The same yard had built the *Kaiserin Auguste Victoria*, a little over two years before. Up until then she was the largest ship ever built in Germany, and it was quite natural that Ballin would turn to Vulcan for the first of his 50,000 tonners. Meanwhile plans were also being drawn up at the great Harland & Wolff yard in Belfast for the second, and perhaps the third, of the new Hapag liners. This yard was in the process of building three huge ships for White Star Line: the *Olympic, Titanic* and *Gigantic.*

Preliminary announcements by Hapag as to size were cautious, and gave only the length between perpendiculars—not the overall length. Statistics for the *Olympic* had been widely circulated, however, and the new German liner would certainly be longer and of greater gross tonnage. But a new beauty was also being built for Cunard, to be named *Aquitania,* and there was a real question in Ballin's mind about her length. It was being suggested that she would be the first ship ever to exceed 900 feet overall. Ballin's new liner had to be larger in every dimension.

Sometime in the winter of 1910-11, Albert Ballin convinced the Kaiser (or vice versa) that the new ship should be named *Imperator.* Ballin quickly shifted his thinking and decided to call the second ship *Europa.* Kaiser Wilhelm promised to officiate at the launch, a major concession of great political importance. Ballin was riding high, and press coverage, particularly in the New World, was most favourable, as witness a December 17, 1910 article in the *Scientific American.* It opened with these words:

> *About once in a decade a new fleet of ocean liners is launched, setting new standard for size, luxury and safety at sea. The great ships which are thought to express the last word in boat building are soon greatly exceeded by their new sisters, and relegated to a second place. The new fleet now under construction (in Germany) surpasses all the great ships which have gone before. To do them justice, we must find a new vocabulary of adjectives for these super-leviathans.*

While precise dates for each step in the evolution of the Ballin Big Three are missing, it can be assumed with reasonable certainty that winning the mail contract from the German government was a key factor in the final plan. Like the brilliant card player he was, Albert

Ballin always managed to have a trump card up his sleeve to offer in return for a new concession. His decision to build the first of the three ships in Germany may have been his winning card in his campaign to garner the Kaiser's enthusiasm for the whole building project, and it is quite possible that the plans he ordered from Harland & Wolff were the bargaining chip he had to use to win the new mail contract essential to his long dreamed of three ship weekly service between Hamburg and New York. The plans were his ace in the hole. Once he had the contract promised, he would agree to build all three ships in Germany, and this is how it worked out. The cost of the design work done at Belfast was little enough compared to the mail contract. We will shortly see how he used the competitive instincts of another great Hamburg shipyard to squeeze an entirely new and ingenious design concept from them, in return for his pledge to give this yard the plumb of building the last two of his Big Three.

New *Imperator* dimensions appeared as the blue prints were finalized. Her gross tonnage was finally estimated at being about 51,969 tons. Her length between perpendiculars was made known: 882.9 feet, and a new extreme beam of 98.3 feet. Her depth of hold was to be 57.1 feet. Her net tonnage was estimated at 23,205 tons and her load displacement would be somewhat above 56,000 tons on a

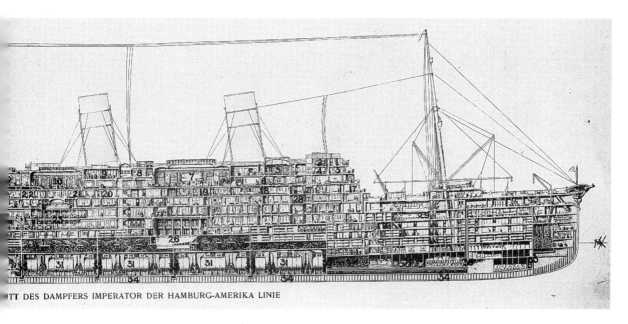

TT DES DAMPFERS IMPERATOR DER HAMBURG-AMERIKA LINIE

draft of 35 feet 6 inches. She would have ten decks, five running for her full length, with two partial decks below the range of machinery compartments, and three superstructure decks above. There would be 12 main watertight bulkheads. While these details were being publicized the world was shocked by the tragic news of the loss of the White Star liner *Titanic*. Around the world, new ships being built were affected by the impact of this disaster. None were more alert to what had to be done than Ballin's team of naval architects. A new inner skin was installed within the shell plating in all the forward holds, extending up to well above the waterline. Photos of this work being done were published around the world. Aft of the new inner hull forward were side bunkers abreast of all the boiler rooms. The ship's original design had called for a six-foot double bottom for the full length. Transverse framing was an added strength factor in the ship's design. There were also longitudinal bulkheads in the engine rooms. The ship's watertight doors could be closed from the bridge.

The question of lifeboats was a burning issue. Old regulations which had permitted the *Titanic* to sail with nothing like enough boats were the target of worldwide criticism. The *Imperator* would have a carrying capacity of more than 5,000 souls, and there would have to be boats for all. To have them all located on the Boat Deck beside the funnels would

Cut-away diagram of the Imperator, *world's largest liner and first to exceed 50,000 tons, number one of Ballin's 'Big Three'. Areas 5, 7 and 10 were two decks high, while 25 and 26 were three decks high, dimensions unheard of up until then.*

have added enormously to the top weight, and it was decided to put more than half of the required lifeboats in recesses aft on the Lower Promenade. Fresh thinking created a design feature using Whelan davits that would swing out from the deck above.

This arrangement, which originated with Albert Ballin's *Imperator,* is used on many of today's largest liners. Not only is the weight of the boats distributed better, but in case of an emergency the ship's companion ways would be relieved of about half of the potential load of passengers rushing for the boats, as they would be in two different locations. It might be noted that the significance of this change was lost to the designers of both Cunard Line, in the case of their new *Aquitania*, and White Star Line, frantically making alterations in the lifeboat arrangements for the *Titanic*'s still unfinished second sister ship, whose name had been quietly changed from *Gigantic* to *Britannic*. As redesigned the *Imperator* would have 83 lifeboats, two of which would be self-propelled.

Four propellers would drive the *Imperator*.

Coaling had to be done on both sides of the ship at the same time, and she was breasted far enough out into the slip so that automatic coal loading lighters could be brought in between the pier and the ship. This photo gives a good close up of the Whelan davits devised to lower the C Deck recessed lifeboats.

The *Olympic* class had only three. The new German ship's propellers would be of 16½ feet in diameter, each having four blades. Direct turbine drive was used. There were 46 water-tube boilers in four 74-foot long boiler rooms. The uptakes from two boiler rooms led to each of the first two huge funnels. The third funnel was a dummy, and here again the Ballin trio were breaking fresh ground. Up until their design, each new class of monster liner had been built with more funnels, until a total of four was accepted as the symbol of the newest and largest. Just exactly how tall the original funnels on the *Imperator* were remains a puzzle. Most sources say they were 69 feet high after they had to be cut down in size, but the

noted maritime historian John Isherwood describes the origin tall funnels as having been 82 feet high from their base on the Boat Deck to their uppermost extremity. We believe Isherwood. It has been written that nine feet was cut off from these. This would mean that the funnels for most of her life were 73 feet high. A close examination of photographs leads me to believe both Isherwood and the 69-foot high final statistic—I think that 13 feet was removed from the tops of these mammoth funnels. It might be added that the tallest funnels ever fitted on to a liner were those built for the Cunarders *Saxonia* and *Ivernia* in 1900. They each had 106-foot single funnels.

Albert Ballin was never satisfied. Although he had commissioned one of the world's best known marine artists to paint an artist's conception of the completed *Imperator*, in 1910, he did the same thing all over again the following year, using an artist who may have been well-known at that time but whose name is now virtually unknown—a man from New Haven, Conn., named A. Bishop. So pleased was Ballin with his finished product that he ordered copies of it to be reproduced in full colour on tin, and sent to agents around the world. It is interesting to note that early versions of this Bishop painting and the Pansing work do not show the stem anchor. Ballin was such a perfectionist that he was continually changing this and improving that. Both of these early renderings also fail to show the lifeboats on the Lower Promenade, and both show E Deck painted white. It might be added here that a decade later Cunard Line employed Artist Bishop to do a new version of this painting, showing the ship as the *Berengaria*. Cunard was so pleased with this work that they reproduced it, also, in the form of a full-colour, tin lithograph.

Albert Ballin decided that he would have to do something to make absolutely sure his new monster steamer was the longest ship in the world. By mid 1911 he probably had learned that the *Aquitania* would be one foot beyond the 900-foot mark. He knew that his blue prints showed an overall length of 909 feet, but a difference of just eight feet was not enough, and so he or one of his designers came up with a bright new thought. Why not add a decorative 'figurehead' to the stem of the new ship? No sooner said than done. A Berlin professor named Bruno Kruse designed the figurehead, which was made of bronze and added 10.3 feet in length to *Imperator*, making

her new overall length 919.3 feet. This length, with figurehead, would stand throughout her life, even though the figurehead was not always to be in place, as will be recorded below.

The figurehead was of an eagle, head thrust forward and topped with an eight-sided Imperial crown. The claws of the eagle rested on a globe, upon which were the words: 'Mein Feld Ist Die Welt,' 'the world is my territory'. Behind the globe were 18 sharply pointed 'rays' extending out from the back of the globe like the rays of the sun. To this day, the *Imperator*'s figurehead has remained one of the most talked about features of her design. I like John Isherwood's summary:

It is true that it was an enormous bird but it was perched on an enormous ship and in my view was neither out of place nor out of proportion. The Germans had every right to be proud of their big ship. I for one would not mind seeing a bronze lion on the stem of the Queen Elizabeth.

American painter Fred Pansing did this artist's conception from blueprints. He added the eagle figurehead after it had been decided upon as a way to make sure the new liner would be longer than the rival Aquitania.

Artist's conceptions of the *Imperator* were being constantly updated to reflect all these changes. New versions of the Bishop and Pansing oil paintings were issued with the eagle figurehead. Frank Bowen, noted British liner authority writing in his classic entitled *A Century of Atlantic Travel* (1930) had this to say:

> If the Olympic *made 1911 essentially a British year, 1912 was equally a German one, for the ship of the year was undoubtedly the Hamburg American* Imperator. *No expense or trouble was spared to make her the most remarkable ship to date as well as the biggest. Her public rooms were the finest ever put afloat.*

May 23, 1912 was a great day in Hamburg. The

The Kaiser smashed the christening bottle by pulling on a silken cord. The spilled champagne can be seen, or maybe it was painted on in this photo sent to the New York Tribune in 1912. Note the massive steelwork and huge timbers under the bow of the Imperator. *(N.Y.* Tribune *and Hapag-Lloyd)*

Kaiser was on hand and he christened the huge new *Imperator*'s hull with every bit of pomp and circumstance Albert Ballin could conjure up. The new ship's prow was looped with wreathes of something like holly. Her upper strake (E Deck) was painted white, as so many of the artists' conceptions had shown. The huge hull weighed 27,000 tons at the moment of launching, even though none of the superstructure was in place. An accident did happen, which, when exaggerated by those who enjoy bringing out the bad side of things, was made to sound most unfortunate. A section of steel chain, possibly from the forward anchor, snapped and flew around 'in the vicinity of the Kaiser's launching platform.' He was not touched. The Kaiser stood alone, high above all others. Below him on another raised level was a large collection of high-hatted dignitaries, fringed by a small group of straw-hatted men and women with highly-decorated and bravely feathered *chapeaux*. A white mass of

Down the ways she goes.

She floats, as tugs take her in hand. (Arnold Kludas)

Note the variety of fancy hats in this view of the official launching party.

rising steam shot up from a tug which was hidden below the crowd of VIPs. Potted palms, that final touch of elegance, were tastefully scattered here and there below the several tasseled canopies.

More details about the ship's engines were released at the time of the launching. Her machinery would consist of four sets of Curtis-A.E.G. Vulcan steam turbines. They would have 62,000 shaft horsepower ahead, and 35,000 astern. She was the first large German liner fitted with turbines.

Her passenger capacity was put at 4,595.

Her two real funnels are in place, the dummy will be erected shortly in this scene at the fitting out berth. (Arnold Kludas)

Workers installing the rudder and port inboard propeller pause to stare at the photographer in this Hamburg American Line photo sent to the N.Y. Tribune in 1912.

She is moved to a floating dry dock for propeller and rudder installation. Note the eagle figurehead and also the mahogany-stained bridge. (Arnold Kludas)

The dirigible Hansa owned by Hamburg American Line pays tribute to the new flagship being coaled for her trials. The tug at the left is taking away an empty coal lighter. Nearly 8,000 tons had to be loaded for each round trip, all done by manual labour.

There was space for 908 in First Class, 972 in Second, 943 in Third and 1,772 in Steerage. Her crew would number 1,180 for a total potential maximum of 5,775. The new estimate for her gross tonnage was set at 52,226 tons and her between-perpendiculars length was confirmed at 882.9 feet. Her normal top speed was given as 23 knots, but it was said that she could probably do 24 under certain circumstances.

The new ship was certainly striking. More details poured out from Hamburg. The First Class Dining Saloon, three decks high when its huge dome was counted, could seat 700. The Main Lounge was another huge room with a large dome.

Trials of a sort were held in April before the ship had steamed down the shallow Elbe. She was officially delivered by the shipyard to Hapag on May 23, 1913. Preparations for the maiden voyage began: there were countless things to be done. The ship was in the news constantly. A contest had been held in Germany to determine the seven 'Wonders of the World', and the *Imperator* was listed as the seventh, following wireless, the Panama Canal, the dirigible, the flying machine, radium and cinematography. Some clever public relations man with Hapag promptly arranged for a photo to be taken of the *Imperator* below the Hamburg American Line's dirigible name *Hansa*. This craft was slightly more than 500 feet in length and made regular air cruises with paying passengers. She had chalked up flights of over 1,000 miles. Her inventor, Count Zeppelin, was predicting that a crossing of the Atlantic might be made before 1913 was over.

An unfortunate incident took place on the trip down the Elbe—the ship ran aground, her 36-foot draft being the deepest of any ship up until then. Fortunately she was not damaged.

Steam from the No. 1 and No. 2 funnel whistles and black smoke make this a superb photo of Imperator as she leaves the yard for her trip down the Elbe to Cuxhaven. The entire bridge face is now white, as it will remain. (Hapag-Lloyd)

A mystery photo, which must have been taken in 1913 because the eagle figurehead is still in place. A tarpaulin covers the forward end of the superstructure, and possibly some repainting was required after the explosion in the engineroom while the ship was at Cuxhaven.

At Cuxhaven, but after the funnels had been cut down to reduce the ship's topheaviness. The figurehead is still in place so this photo must have been taken late in 1913.

This almost identical shot is different, because the figurehead is no longer there. All the Boat Deck lifeboats are in place once again. (Arnold Kludas)

Pulled off, she completed the run without further delay. Then there was a more serious episode—one of her boilers exploded. One report said that five crewmen were killed. Few facts leaked out, but the explosion was blamed on carelessness on the part of workmen at Cuxhaven. The maiden voyage had been set to begin on May 24, and it was postponed until June 10. The delay was most embarrassing to Albert Ballin, but fortunately for him and for Hapag, the Kaiser's enthusiasm for the new ship was not diminished, and each new accident was taken in stride. We have a first-hand account of the maiden voyage from J. Bernard Walker, writing in the *Scientific American*. He had been invited aboard for the maiden crossing.

At the first sight of such a ship one fails to grasp its magnitude. The first thing that strikes the visitor is the unusual height between decks, which in the case of several is from 11 to 12 feet. If the ship were to be placed in Broadway it would be necessary to cut 18 feet beyond the building line on each side of that thoroughfare for a length of four city blocks, and the roof of the topmost tier of staterooms and assembly halls would extend far above the roof-line of the six and seven story buildings erected in the pre-skyscraper period.

Two days out, under pressure of strong winds, the 'ship assumed a slight angle of heel.' This was the first reference to what was to become recognized as a major weakness—her stability. The great ship was topheavy. Passengers were also alarmed at the way she 'hung on to her roll.' Instead of recovering quickly, she would remain over this way or that much longer than other ships, giving those aboard

Commodore Hans Ruser, Commander-in-Chief of the Imperator, *smiling as he demonstrates how the engine-room telegraph works. He would also have the distinction of commanding the* Vaterland *and the* Bismarck, *to follow.*

One of the several captains serving under Commodore Ruser. Note the open bridge. This was a tradition of that era and it meant very, very cold working conditions in winter. There was an inner, enclosed wheelhouse.

A boat drill was one of the first routines gone through. This photo was probably taken in the North Sea, as the style of the small vessel under sail on the horizon suggests. The lifeboats are stained mahogany at this point. Later they would be painted white. Note the girders holding up the dome over the Lounge, just aft of funnel No. 1.

an uneasy feeling. When she entered New York her pilot was Capt. George Seeth, Sr. As he boarded her he noticed she had a decided list to port. A while later, when he ordered 'easy right rudder', he sensed that she had finally straightened up. Everyone on the bridge breathed a sigh of relief, but then, as she completed her turn into Ambrose Channel, she listed over to starboard and stayed that way. As he remembered, anything that was loose fell, and some passengers even lost their footing. There was something definitely wrong. She docked, however, without a slip, entering Pier 1, Hoboken with the help of 11 tugs with ease. Her progress up the harbour had been one that would have given Albert Ballin, had he been aboard, much cause for pride

and satisfaction. She was greeted with a steady series of whistle salutes and cheers. Needless to say a horde of ship news reporters were aboard the cutter that came out from the Barge Office at the Battery, and their stories made the front pages of all the major daily newspapers, along with large photographs of the monster new ship passing in front of the Woolworth and Singer buildings. Commodore Hans Ruser was delighted with the reception.

The *Imperator* completed her maiden voyage from Cherbourg to New York in six days, five hours and twelve minutes. She brought with her 3,014 passengers, 323 in First Class, 251 in Second and 2,440 in Third. Hapag had hired Brown & Dawson, photographers of Stamford, Conn., to cover the maiden arrival for posterity. Perhaps the most famous of all the photos taken of the maiden arrival is that snapped from a boat off Jersey City. The huge vessel is pictured with the Woolworth building rising on Manhattan Island just forward of her bow, only partly obscured by the ship's stem. Cargo booms are slung out ready to be used in unloading. A huge German flag at the

Guests and company officials watch coaling from the top deck. Note the many-windowed public room aft on the Promenade Deck. This would be entirely removed before many months to help clear up the stability problem.

Note the slight list to port in this view of the inbound Imperator passing the Woolworth Building. In the aftermath of the Titanic disaster, the ship boasted a huge searchlight low on the foremast.

With her stem anchor out and at 'the ready', the new Hapag flagship turns towards Hoboken to enter her slip. The two-stacked liner behind her is the Amerika, built for Hapag by Harland & Wolff only seven years before, but now outclassed.

stern whips to the breeze. No smoke is visible from the two forward funnels. A slight list to port is evident. Another outstanding picture shows the *Imperator* coming up to her Hoboken pier. The dock has an extension at its outer end to make it longer, and this is jam-packed with people, standing so close to the edge that any movement in the crowd would surely force half a dozen into the water. The Hapag house magazine summarized the reception at New York in glowing terms: 'Nothing

No. 3 funnel, the dummy. This is at New York after completion of the maiden voyage. Officials are entering the ship from the two government craft breasted outside the after sideport.

could diminish the general feeling of gladness which indeed among the Americans was so hearty and unrestrained that it rose to almost frenzied, jubilant applause.' The same journal, in a gentle reproof to the British for their tongue-in-cheek sympathy for the ship's maiden voyage problems, hailed the Americans as being

> *entirely free from all illiberal narrow-mindedness, recognizing quite justly the eminently peaceful significance of the Hamburg-Amerika Line's new weapon of warfare which, though aimed against the hostile powers of Nature, was nevertheless designed for the safety and protection of friendly intercourse and peaceful traffic between nations, and for the blessings and prosperity arising from their interchange of goods.*

One untoward episode marred the first visit to New York. There was a small fire aboard,

which, because she was the world's largest ship, made all the front pages. It was in her passenger quarters aft, and hoses were directed down the hatch covers in that area. Over-eager fireboats poured tons of water aboard, through her port-holes and down the after hatches. She already had a slight list to starboard, and with so much water pumped aboard this list increased quite drastically. The fireboats were ordered to stop and, fortunately for all concerned, obeyed the order. The fire was put out and preparations were made for the return crossing.

Her maiden eastbound crossing had a large passenger list. There were 704 in First Cabin, a figure that probably was a record. Another

Photographers concentrate on the eagle figurehead, which seems to have taken on a living character. The docking officer stands on his little bow 'bridge' directing things, while the company houseflag whips in the breeze between the figurehead's two huge wings. Note the stack of the Hoboken ferry berthed at the terminal down river.

The ship is listing to starboard, as lines hold her into her Hoboken pier. A fire has been discovered in a hold far aft. Note the longshoremen moving a hose on the string piece on the lower level of the pier to the left: the eagle figurehead has taken on a frightened look.

The list is worse due to water the fire fighters have poured into the ship, but the fire is out. White-uniformed officers inspect things from the pierhead roof. In years to come, the steel bulwarks on the foredeck will be replaced, for some unfathomable reason, by railings.

Fireboats remain ready to help, should the fire start up again. Coal lighters are already alongside. The Amerika's twin stacks and four masts can be seen at the north side of Pier 1. A small excursion boat passes.

533 signed up at the 45 Broadway Hapag North American headquarters to sail to Europe in Second Class. Third and Steerage had a total of 1,095, less than half the figure for these categories on the first westbound passage. The total that sailed home with her was 2,332.

Just when the questions of stability and boiler adjustments were faced I do not know. The *Imperator* continued to make transatlantic trips, doing very well. The 3,646 she carried westbound on her third voyage was her largest passenger list—ever, and may be one of if not the largest passengers list by a single vessel in the history of North Atlantic travel. It might also be noted that the First Class passenger list of 859 for the September 17 New York arrival may well be the largest number of passengers to arrive in this class in port history, and certainly was the *Imperator*'s largest First Class list.

The eagle figurehead came to an abrupt and sad end. On one of the 1913 crossings it was badly damaged by wave action, as any sailor would have been able to predict. Its remnant parts were quietly removed and replaced by a much less ornate gilded iron scroll design

Fire hoses are limp now that the crisis is over. This shows how they were aimed down into the hold, via one of the after hatches on D Deck.

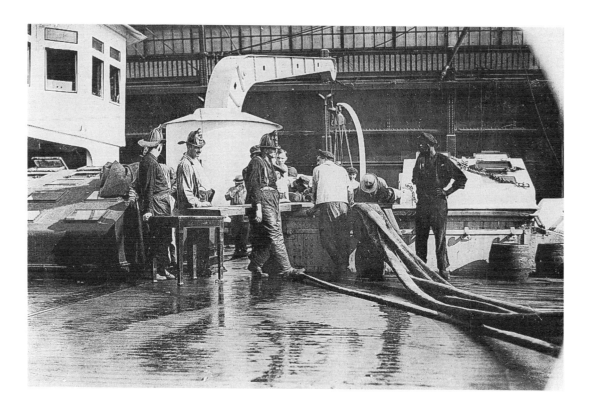

A magnificent view showing the shortened funnels against the New York skyline. Many wrote that they thought the ship looked better this way.
I prefer the original outline with the taller funnels.
A 36 in enlargement of this picture hung for 60 years in 45 Broadway. (Arnold Kludas)

Outward bound with a new bow decoration similar to that of the Vaterland. At this point the stability problem was so well in hand that plans were being considered to move the D Deck lifeboats up to the Boat Deck. (Arnold Kludas)

An artist's conception of the Winter Garden and the raised Ritz Carlton Restaurant, sent in 1912 to the N.Y. Tribune.

How the Ritz Carlton actually looked. It was run by the same management that ran the restaurants of this name in London and New York. Lighter cane furniture was substituted for the heavy pieces shown here, when the ship's stability problem became evident.

Another 76-year-old 8 x 10 artist's conception. It shows the First Class Lounge with its elegant stage for concerts, as first conceived by Hapag interior decorators.

And the Lounge as it became a reality, even more handsome than the concept. Note the white marble bust of Kaiser Wilhelm II.

The artist's conception of the three-deck-high First Class Dining Saloon on Imperator.

A heroic-sized painting of the Kaiser, done to decorate the main stairway on A Deck.

The three-deck-high Pompeian Swimming Pool. The Ballin Big Three had the finest indoor pools ever designed for any liners, before or after.

The First Class Smoking Room, forward on A Deck. The sculptured frieze above the panelling is made of tooled leather.

on either side of the stem, similar to that which the second of Ballin's Big Three would have.

By now, however, the war was almost upon them. Albert Ballin must have been torn to shreds, with pressures of his own due to his tremendous building programme, with disappointments because of the way the Kaiserin was isolating the Kaiser from him, and with tensions because of the rising war fever in Germany.

Ahead would be some great moments. He would watch the completion of the second of his 'Big Three', which would be named *Vaterland* instead of *Europa*, due to another political compromise. He would experience the joy of reading proofs of big Hapag ads aimed at American travellers and hailing '*Imperator* and *Vaterland*—World's Largest Ships, Fastest to the Continent.' And he would see his third ship launched on June 20, 1914. She, too, would be renamed for political reasons, at the last minute, being christened *Bismarck*. He would see very large passenger lists carried on the six round trips of the *Imperator* in 1914 and the three and a half voyages made by the *Vaterland*. But he probably knew that disaster of untoward size lay ahead, and that his worst fears would soon be realized.

The *Imperator* spent half of November, all of December, January, February and the first part of March, 1914 at Cuxhaven. She was given a complete going over and emerged a much better ship. The stability problems seem to have been cleared up, and there were few complaints about her turbines after this rebuilding. The reduction in size of her funnels favoured her overall appearance—she looked longer, lower and sleeker. What was perhaps lost in her original impression of huge size, was replaced in a finer feeling of proportion. The *Imperator* was a most handsome and powerful looking vessel. She arrived at New York on March 19 on the first of her six 1914 round trips, carrying 2,693 passengers. There were only 371 in First and 334 in Second, but Third and Steerage had 1,988, a fine list. She was under the command of Captain Theo Kier.

A striking photograph was taken from the Jersey City shore as the *Imperator* slowly and majestically steamed up the Hudson. It was a full broadside, and it was snapped just as

the pride of Hamburg was passing the Singer skyscraper and the Woolworth tower, the world's tallest building for many years. The *Imperator* carried 2,980 home, sailing out of New York on March 21. Her second westbound crossing brought 3,118 to the New World. She returned with 2,150. Arriving on May 9, completing her third 1914 westbound passage she had 518 in First, 336 in Second and 2,431 in Third and Steerage for a grand total of 3,285. This fine passenger list was surpassed by the 3,563 that she took out on her third eastbound crossing. Her fourth westbound total came to 2,837, and again she had a very large list sailing home—3,394. Her fifth and sixth crossings saw her do well but set no new records. Her last departure from New York as a German liner took place on July 18. On her last three voyages she sailed in company with the new *Vaterland*.

On one of her last westward passages in 1914 the *Imperator* averaged 23.6 knots, a most respectable speed when it is remembered that Hapag was supposed to be disinterested in setting new speed records. The Blue Riband of the Atlantic was held at that time by Cunard's sleek *Mauretania,* with a passage made in September, 1909 from Daunt's Rock to Sandy Hook which averaged 26.06 knots.

On the last eastbound crossing of the *Imperator*, she passed the *Vaterland* in mid-Atlantic. We wonder whether any passenger had the opportunity to take a photo from the one Hapag monster showing the other passing? The *Imperator* arrived at Hamburg just about as the *Vaterland* reached New York. The *Vaterland* was then laid up, being put in charge of a small staff of watchmen. Albert Ballin kept hoping that somehow he would get the *Vaterland* back and could complete the *Bismarck*, so that his dream of a weekly Hapag service could actually happen. But tragedies can not be rewritten with happy endings.

At the war's end a new life lay ahead for the long-idle *Imperator*. Gone were the glory days of Hamburg American Line, gone with Kaiser—he would spend the rest of his sad life in Holland. And gone was Albert Ballin. He had died shortly after Germany surrendered, a victim of the war just as much as any of the millions of innocents who had been

The Imperial Suite — a view from the bedroom into the private verandah. There were two suites of this type on the Imperator.

One of the sitting rooms in the Imperial Suite. The suite included nine rooms. Original paintings were on the walls.

slaughtered. But his three great ships all survived, and each would have colourful lives in the years ahead. On April 27, 1919, the *Imperator* sailed for the last time ever out of Hamburg. She would never return. She steamed to Brest in France, where she was tied up awaiting delivery to the United States to help return American troops.

On May 4 she became the USS *Imperator* and was taken over by Rear Admiral Casey Morgan, then a Captain. Capt. R. Gracie White was made her commander. Within a ten-day period she was fitted out to transport 9,000 troops and 1,400 first class passengers.

May 23, 1919, was a big day in the story of the *Imperator*. She made her second 'maiden arrival', this time flying the US flag as an American troopship. 'Back after five years' was the three-column headline on the front page of the *New York Tribune*. As an American troopship, the *Imperator* carried 161 passengers to Europe, 147 wounded home and

The Kaiser's Study in the Imperial Suite. Note the fireplace to the right. Wall-to-wall carpeting was a new feature on ships.

The drawing room of a private suite on the Imperator, a photo sent world-wide in 1912.

An artist's conception showing the 'dining room of a suite' on Imperator. Although this was not specified as being the Imperial Suite, it probably was.

Still another conception — the bedroom of one of the suites. Cabins like this had their own private toilet and bath.

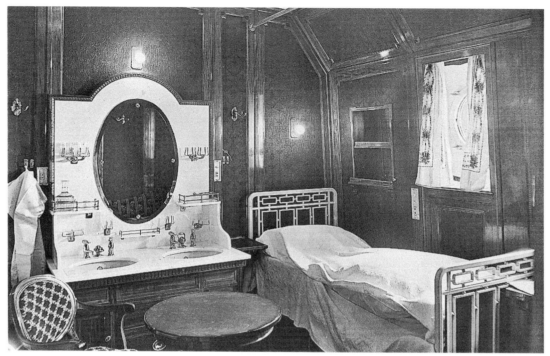

This is a regular First Class cabin on the Imperator,
one of two-dozen sepia-toned photos hand-pasted in
an elegant brochure of 1913. Note the electric
sockets on either side of the marble sinks.

This ship's gymnasium, First Class. Second Class also
had one. Space does not permit us to show Second,
Third and Steerage public rooms and cabins.

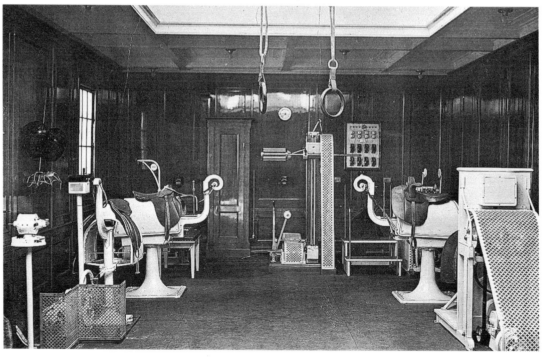

The headline for this photo was 'Back After Five Years'. Here is the USS Imperator, *troops crowding her forward areas and giving the ship a list to starboard as they stare at the skyline of New York. This photo was published May 23, 1919, by the N.Y. Tribune.*

28,030 troops in three and a half turn arounds. On August 10, 1919 the Navy released her to the US Shipping Board, which assumed control over her at her berth in Hoboken. Major stories around the world heralded the announcement made on September 20, 1919, that the *Imperator* was to be assigned to Cunard Line.

One news account began: 'The mighty *Imperator* will fly the flag of the Cunard Line. The former Hamburg-American liner has been turned over to that company for management and will be delivered in New York sometime next week.' The transfer was delayed for a month because the British government had seized several oil tankers owned by the Standard Oil Company of the United States, but flying the German flag. The Shipping Board attempted to force their return by announcing that they would hold the big former German liner until the tankers were released by the

A view at sunset as tugs assist Imperator *into the Cunard pier on the Manhattan side of the Hudson. Published 7 December, 1919, the photo also shows 'the shadowy form of the other ex-German ocean giant,* Leviathan, *across the river.'* Vestris *(bottom right) was an ill-fated liner on charter to Cunard at the time, making transatlantic voyages.*

British, but the British would not budge. Their position was supported by President Wilson and on November 21 the US Shipping Board surrendered the steamship *Imperator* to the British Ministry of Shipping.

The turning-over of the *Imperator* was described with plenty of good detail in the *New York Herald* of Tuesday, November 25, 1919:

Another chapter in the story of the crushing of Germany as a merchant marine power was written yesterday when the mammoth passenger steamship Imperator, *was given to Cunard. A bugle call marked the lowering of the Stars and Stripes. The flag was carefully gathered in the arms of an American sailor, with the caretaking crew of 200 men lined up on the after deck. The North side of Pier 54, of the Cunard Line had been made ready for the* Imperator. *Capt. Miller, Cunard Marine Superintendent, and Capt. Palfrey, the assistant superintendent, were on the deck of the* Imperator *when possession was relinquished by the American government. So was Capt. Charles Appleton Smith, who will command the* Imperator *for Cunard. Capt. J.E. McCarthy, Sandy Hook pilot was in charge of towing the huge ship across the Hudson. The passage across the river required about 30 minutes. While Pier 54 was long enough to safely berth the* Imperator, *with about 20 feet to spare, the steamship towered high above the pier structure and she can be seen many blocks away.*

An illustration of the general excitement that the first sailing of the RMS *Imperator* generated may be seen in a quaint limerick written by a guest at the famous Hotel Plaza. It was published in the *New York Herald* on December 11, 1919, sailing day. It was written by Major the Right Hon. William Henry Edmond De Ver Sheaffe Pery, the fourth Earl of Limerick. RMS *Imperator* looked superb in the R.T. Phillips photo published on December 12, 1919, by the *New York Daily News*. It was a bow view and showed tugs pushing her out of

Pier 54. The article began: 'After several days of delay due to an investigation of the quality of coal she had taken into her bunkers, the great steamship *Imperator*, once the pride of German hearts, steamed yesterday for Liverpool, flying the British flag and under the control of the Cunard Line.' There were 2,741 passengers aboard when 'with whistles blowing and the sun glistening on her newly painted red and black funnels, she backed out into the river from West 14th St. A passing tugboat and two barges got in the way, but the big vessel slowed down until the little craft scurried out of danger.' She took 11 days to make the crossing, being four days behind schedule because of dirty boilers and bad coal.

The *Imperator* was laid up in England for two months, sailing again for New York from Liverpool on February 21, 1920. The Cunard Line had drastically altered her capacity, announcing that she would carry 970 in First, 830 in Second and 1,000 in Tourist. Vast areas at the bown and stern which had originally been for Steerage were left unused at this point. She was being operated by Cunard, but was still owned by the Government of Great Britain. Her first eastbound crossing ended in something of a minor disaster at Southampton. She arrived there with a noticeable list, said to be due to a leak caused by a faulty ash-ejector.

Still running under the name of *Imperator*, the big vessel was by no means restored to the status that Cunard would have wished for. Everything was being done in a 'make do' kind of way, things were in a state of flux. Cunard's great new building programme was about to start, producing a whole fleet of moderate-sized liners. An October 16, 1920, piece in the *Nautical Gazette* illustrates the dilemma faced by Cunard. It began: 'When the *Imperator* and the *Kaiserin Auguste Victoria* were allocated to Cunard for operation, it was understood that they would be used for seven round trips and then turned back to the British Ministry of Shipping .... In any case it is regarded as probable that the *Imperator* will be laid up this winter owing to the high price of coal.' Another American maritime monthly ran a thought-piece on November 20, 1920, in which it was predicted that the *Imperator* might become a

floating hotel at a dockside, 'as it is too costly to operate as a passenger carrier.' This story added that no bids had been received by the British Ministry of Shipping for the giant liner. Nevertheless, she continued sailing, with round trip crossings in November and December. Cunard is said to have lost as much as $50,000 on a single trip of the *Imperator*. One source summarized by saying that efforts to operate the captured liner at a profit had been 'disappointing in the extreme.' The 'experienced companies,' it was added, 'are no longer desirous of holding the extremely large vessels.'

All this negative talk may possibly have had a purpose. Cunard and White Star were in the middle of negotiations with the British government to acquire the two huge Ballin liners. It would not have been wise to have let the powers that be think they might be profitable. And so it turned out in the Spring of 1921 that the two great transAtlantic liner companies in Great Britain jointly bought *Imperator* and *Bismarck*. It was an unusual arrangement, to say

With the name Imperator *on her bow – touched in crudely – in this photo, the great ship is backing out of her Cunard pier. She has Cunard red and black smokestacks for the first time. Look closely and you will see she is lacking her stem anchor. Something must have happened to it during her months as the* USS Imperator.

the least, each company owning half of one of the ships. Cunard was given full operating responsibility for the *Imperator*, and White Star for the *Bismarck*. This arrangement would continue for ten years.

The *Imperator* made two voyages to New York early in 1921 with relatively small passenger lists. As early as February 13 advertisements began to appear featuring the great ship under a new name. She would be called *Berengaria*. Cunard's naming accouncement pointed out that the selection was a departure from their customary habit of calling their vessels after provinces of the Roman Empire. The original Berengaria had been a daughter of Snacho VI of Navarre. She was married to Richard I of England, Richard the Lion Heart.

The liner sailed on April 16, 1921, her first voyage under this new name.

The times were very bad for North Atlantic shipping, but Cunard was in business 'for keeps' and their management knew that good times followed bad times. In mid August it was announced that the *Berengaria* would be taken in hand after her October round trip, and given a complete refit, including converting her into an oil burner. It was stated that the conversion would 'add materially to her speed.' The *Berengaria* arrived at the Tyne on October 31, 1921. Her refit would take six months. She was to be dry-docked in the famous Trafalgar dry dock, but it was not quite large enough. To

Cunard renamed her Berengaria. This outstanding photo by Edwin Levick shows her in the Lower Bay, Manhattan. She is now in the peak of condition. Has any other ship ever looked so impressive? As one of her officers would say 'even the dogs who travelled on her were aristocrats of the dog world'.

make her fit it was necessary to cut a large 'V'-shaped notch in the end where her bow would be. Even with this, there was only 18 inches between her rudder and the dry dock caisson. The docking was carried out by John I. Thornycroft & Co, with the help of employees of Cunard Line, who had to be used because a strike was in progress. The ship was in her tenth year of life at this point.

External changes were minimal. The last three lifeboats housed on the Lower

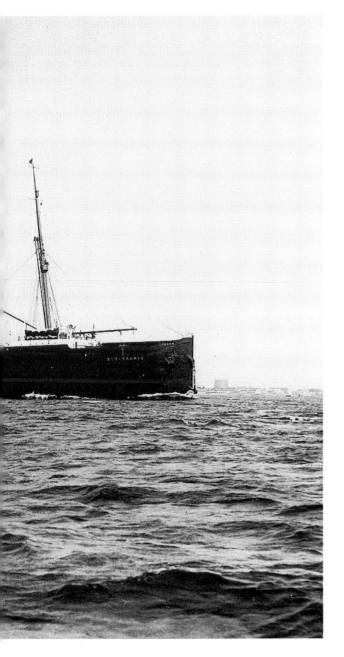

Promenade Deck on each side were moved up to the Boat Deck. The boats on the short pool deck far aft were removed. About 1,000 tons of new steel work was required, and the engine repair work proved most successful. She proved it with two exceptionally fast passages that year: a westward crossing at 23.27 knots average, and an eastward passage at 23.79 knots. For the next 16 years her service was almost continuous.

Tourism saved Cunard Line. The fleet of newly-built Cunarders proved to be a good investment. Travel across the Atlantic was on the upswing in 1923, and Cunard's Queen of the Fleet was the *Berengaria*. The fact that she had only three funnels instead of four was a point in her favour, as it made her look more modern. The company began putting out expensive brochures about her, hailing her really magnificent public rooms. Lovely as she was, the *Aquitania* could not quite match the high-ceilinged Main Lounge, Ritz Carlton Restaurant, Winter Garden and First Class Dining Saloon on the *Berengaria*.

Fine pen and ink drawings of the *Berengaria* were commissioned from the American artist Fred Hoertz. The earliest of the brochures showed old photos of the liner, with the Hapag funnels retouched. The ship's huge passenger capacity was described in this way: 'The population of the *Berengaria* is over 4,000 souls. It is truly a city—a city of the sea. A crew of more than one thousand, and over three thousand passengers—these hundreds of people live together on the great ship for a week without crowding, without half of them ever meeting.'

A handsome four-page *Berengaria* folder put out in 1923 has a fine photo of the liner being towed from a shipyard by two paddle wheel tugs. On the back page the complete 24-liner fleet of that day is listed, with the *Berengaria* leading. She had finally been accepted. Late in this same year Cunard issued another *Berengaria* brochure, 24 pages long and featuring full page, sepia tone photos. Its cover was a black and white pen sketch of the ship by Fred Hoertz.

Europe was slowly returning to something like normal following the devastation of the First World War. A surge of new emigrants was sailing for the New World. The impact of this

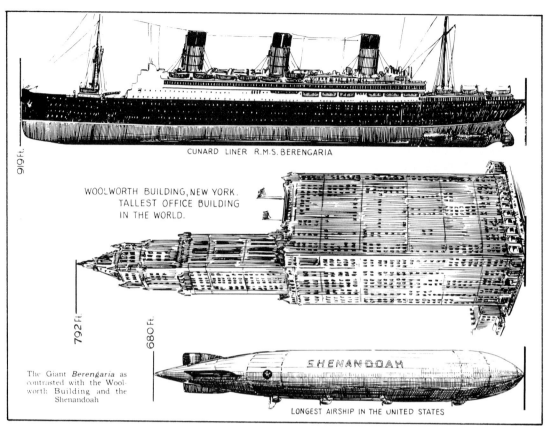

CUNARD LINER R.M.S. BERENGARIA

919 Ft.

WOOLWORTH BUILDING, NEW YORK.
TALLEST OFFICE BUILDING
IN THE WORLD.

792 Ft.

680 Ft.

SHENANDOAH

The Giant *Berengaria* as
contrasted with the Wool-
worth Building and the
Shenandoah

LONGEST AIRSHIP IN THE UNITED STATES

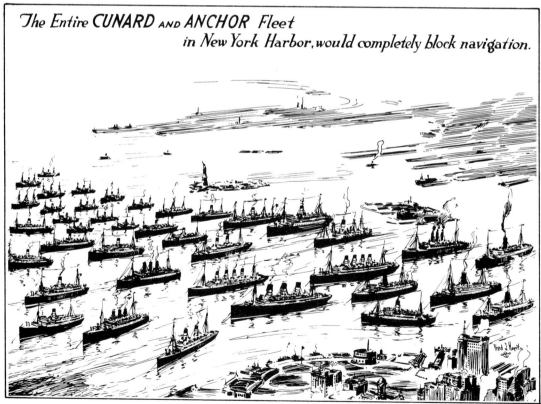

The Entire CUNARD *and* ANCHOR *Fleet*
in New York Harbor, would completely block navigation.

happy development may be seen in the passenger totals for the *Berengaria* for 1923. On 14 westbound trips she carried 19,742 passengers, 7,909 in Tourist and Third Classes. She made 15 eastbound passages carrying only 10,165, but the tourist trade with the Old World was also developing rapidly. All in all 1923 was a good year for Cunard. The following year was even better, although passenger totals were only slightly higher. The 1924 class-by-class figures were reversed, very much in favour of the Cunard treasury. Instead of Third and Tourist making up the bulk of the passenger lists, the *Berengaria* carried more than double these lower categories in First Class: 7,733 compared to 3,191 on westbound crossings. Eastbound it was almost as good, with

Two pages from an interesting brochure called 'Cunard Comparisons'. The artwork was by an up-and-coming young American marine artist named Fred. J. Hoertz. How many of the fine Cunard and Anchor line ships in the lower drawing can you identify, gentle reader?

Silhouetted. Press photographers returning on a tug after Berengaria sailed for Europe — two are shown on the stern deck of their tug, captured in the picture by a third. The hazy day did not dull the sunlight on the harbour.

First Class passengers numbering 6,413 in contrast to 4,226 who went either Third or Tourist. Cunard's publicity department and all the expensive brochures produced in 1922 were paying off.

Perhaps this was what prompted the company, in February, 1924, to go all out with one of the most extravagant booklets ever produced by any ship line. It was eight inches wide and 18 inches high, and filled with original sketches and superb ship paintings, all reproduced in colour. Its heavy, almost cardboard weight, front cover carried the title: *Cunard Line—Eight Decades of Progress*, and the booklet was printed for initial use at the British Empire Exhibition at Wembley.

Soon the *Berengaria* came to be known for the wealthy passengers she attracted. All sorts of distinguished voyagers were pictured in *The*

This view, taken in 1922, shows how Cunard began moving the C Deck lifeboats to the Boat Deck at this point. Look between the two gangplanks and you can see that three of them are still in their lower deck recesses. The others have been raised and the space they occupied is now a lower promenade deck.

Another sunset — showing Berengaria, inbound, passing the Statue of Liberty. The shadows suggest the time would have been early evening. The Titanic-disaster-inspired searchlight is still on its platform on the foremast, showing this to be still in the mid 1920s.

At this sailing Mrs William Howard Taft was 'lost' aboard and delayed the departure 15 minutes. Wet snow blanketed the ship. It looks as if the Leviathan, upper left, is getting ready to move away from her winter berth in Hoboken. Note that all the lifeboats are now up on Boat Deck.

*This appeared in the N.Y. Tribune, August 30, 1924.
It shows small boats swarming about the incoming
liner with the Prince of Wales aboard. The yacht
Black Watch, whose two low stacks may be seen at
the lower right, took the Prince ashore.*

Cunarder, the company house organ, posing
on deck in front of *Berengaria* lifebelts. On
August 29, 1924, the Prince of Wales sailed
on the *Berengaria*, to attend the polo matches
at Meadow Brook, Long Island, and would
return on the *Aquitania*. A newsphoto of his
arrival showed the intent observer that Cunard
had removed the last of the Lower Promenade
Deck lifeboats. All the boats were by then on
the Boat Deck—there was clearly no longer
any problem of stability.

*An advertisement published on
December 15, 1924, offered an
'Automobile Route to Europe Via Cunard
Ocean Highway.' It would cost only
$441 'complete . . . covers car
transportation both ways, crating—
duties—customs—permits—plates and
licences for a 125 inch wheelbase—5
passenger—open car . . . also American*

*and foreign club dues and maps . . . .
We attend to everything. You do nothing
but drive your car to Pier 54, North
River . . . . Cheaper than touring at
home. Wonderful roads. Easy driving.
See more—learn more.*

On one crossing in 1925, the *Berengaria*
docked on Saturday morning instead of Friday night, because she had been called upon
to rescue an injured sailor from a freighter and
had had to retrace her course by 20 miles. A
photograph published in the *New York Tribune* showed her lifeboat bringing the seaman
alongside. A powerful pen sketch of the *Berengaria* being swept by 50-foot waves on a
November eastbound crossing was carried by
the *New York Times* on November 22, 1925.
Fifty passengers were injured 'and six were
bruised', the caption reported. Fifteen westbound crossings were made this year with
15,843 passengers carried. Sixteen eastbound
trips took 19,449 people back to Europe, a new
record for the *Berengaria*. In 1926 her passenger totals were slightly less, due to her
schedule which allowed just 15 crossings each
way. Her First Class carryings continued to

be almost double the number carried in Third Class.

The year 1927 saw the *Berengaria* carry more passengers than she had ever carried before. True, there were none of the 3,000-plus loads she had carried as the *Imperator*, but her 35,292 total was a new post-war record. And it was a record even though she made only 29 crossings, compared to 31 in 1925 when she had set her earlier best year mark. One rough passage this year produced a thin little yarn which may well be remembered. A writer for the *New Yorker* magazine interviewed John Masefield and his wife, who had arrived on this *Berengaria* crossing. She said: 'It was too uppy-downy, and John was ill.' This was enough to excite the *New Yorker*'s correspondent to write a brief parody of Masefield's famous poem that begins 'I Must Go Down to the Seas Again . . .' It began:

> '*I must go down to the seas again,*
> *where the billows romp and reel*
> *So all I ask is a large ship that rides on*
> *an even keel,*
> *And a mild breeze and a broad deck*
> *with a slight list to leeward,*
> *And a clean chair and a snug nook and*
> *a nice, kind steward.*

New York's popular mayor James J. Walker, sailed on the *Berengaria* in the summer of 1927, arriving in his Rolls Royce, which boasted a large letter 'W' on its licence plate. Strutting down to the gangplank, the Mayor was met by Sir Arthur Rostron, the ship's new master, famed for rescuing the survivors of the *Titanic*. Aboard, Walker held a press conference in the ship's Main Lounge, as his Imperial Suite was not large enough to house all the reporters and photographers. He made a broadcast over Station WNYC and then enjoyed a wild and woolly *bon voyage* party. One accompanying newsman said that during the crossing it was not always clear who was the master, Walker or Captain Rostron.

The year 1928 saw 37,060 passengers carried by the *Berengaria*, her best total up to then and thereafter. She made 31 crossings and First Class totals remained higher than those of any other category. One colourful passenger this year was Anastasia, daughter of Czar Nicholas II, who was to spend her sad life trying to convince her relatives that she really was the

A drawing of what Berengaria looked like in a storm — done by a London Daily Express staff artist and published with a news story about the gale on November 22, 1925. Not bad, either.

A N.Y. Tribune *arrival photo showing the first of Ballin's Big Three docking early in the morning after a stormy passage with many notables and six million dollars aboard. Heavy fog held her down the bay 16 hours. The photo is magnificent as a display of steam and smoke over quiet water.*

Czar's youngest offspring. She had cabin 419. It was said she was coming to America to have bayonet scars removed from her face. Serge Rachmaninoff, the famed composer, who was among the other passengers, had acknowledged her legitimacy from the start. Met by a large group of ship news reporters and photographers, Anastasia was quoted by one of these as saying that the *Berengaria* was 'nothing like the Czar's yacht *Standart*.'

Sir Arthur Rostron was named Commodore of Cunard Line on July 28, 1929. The *Berengaria* was at last flagship of the entire Cunard fleet, and the Commodore's pennant flew from her main truck. The *Berengaria* enjoyed another splendid year. Her passenger total for 15 eastbound and 15 westbound crossings was 36,853—barely under the previous record of 37,060. A new rudder was needed for the *Berengaria*, and this was fitted in mid February. The year is remembered throughout the western world for the Wall Street crash in October. Some time before that, the International Telephone and Telegraph company had begun a ship-to-shore service aboard the *Berengaria*. With such a facility available, a 36-year-old Wall Street wizard, Michael J. Meecham, rented space on the *Berengaria* in the fall of the year, and set up the world's first stockbroker's office on a transatlantic liner. A fine book has been written about this bit of social history and the traumatic experiences Meecham's patrons and staff endured during the week of the Wall Street crash, during the mid October crossing from Cherbourg to New York. The book is entitled *The Berengaria Exchange*, and is by Paul Knapp.

With the Depression getting steadily worse, the year 1930 saw nothing much to be cheerful about on the Atlantic. The *Berengaria* made only 12 westbound crossings and 13 eastbound.

Her passenger total was way down—off by over one-third.

Her Senior First Officer for considerable periods was Capt. Harry Grattidge, who would later be Commodore of the Cunard Line. His autobiography has this most negative comment: 'She was a ship of gloomy panelled majesty, hard to handle, clumsy and Teutonic, a creation of industry without pretensions to beauty.' Capt. Grattidge's comments extended to her passengers: 'Everybody on the *Berengaria*, even the dogs, were socially prominent.' And here he pointed to the famous Rin-Tin-Tin, Jr., whose owner had a First Class ticket but lived with his dog on the Third Class Deck. And Gertrude Lawrence's dog, in whose behalf the noted actress would violate all rules by exercising it on deck each morning. Grattidge apprehended her in this very act one morning and 'escorted her in grim silence back to the kennels.'

A six-day cruise to Halifax was offered by the *Berengaria* in the summer of 1930. It had originally been listed as a cruise to nowhere, and the *New York Times* quoted shipping sources as fearing that the ship 'would be the scene of drinking orgies.' The American Steamship Owners Association objected to cruises to nowhere by foreign-flag ships, saying that they violated the spirit of the coastwise laws. Quite a flap developed, but the American protest achieved nothing. In mid October the Cunard Line announced that the *Berenagaria* would be laid up early in November for extensive turbine overhauling and interior refurbishing. She would get new oil tanks to double her capacity, so that in the future she could buy oil at New York for a round trip, increasing her economy of operation. As winter fell the company made known that the overhaul would take longer than anticipated, and that the *Mauretania* would be speeded up so she could take *Berengaria*'s February 25, 1931 westbound sailing. The flagship, however, would be ready to sail on March 21, from Southampton. On her last day in dry dock, a full set of houseflags was hoisted aboard *Berengaria*. A brave sight she was indeed.

On March 21, 1931, the *Berengaria* sailed from Southampton on her first voyage of the new year. She had a new master, Capt. Edgar Britten, formerly of the *Franconia*. He replaced Sir Arthur Rostron, who retired. Capt. Britten already had many honours, and would go on to become perhaps Britain's most famous liner master. His autobiography, entitled *A Million Ocean Miles* contains many grand stories. The Depression became even worse in 1931, only ten voyages were made by the *Berengaria*. Her passenger totals were way below the poor showing of 1930. One eastbound passage ended with some excitement, though. She sailed on March 31 from New York with 139 in First Class. Second Class had only 49, Tourist had 78 and there were 88 in Third. Approaching Southampton on Tuesday, April 7, the ship ran aground. Tugs came to her help and all but 75 of her passengers were taken ashore by tender. It must have been a hectic operation, and those who stayed aboard for the night displayed much wisdom. At about 3 am the next morning she was dragged off the mud, but the fog was so thick that she hove to until daylight before proceeding into port.

With regular passenger traffic so low, Cunard turned with a will to short cruises. The famous 'Big Three' (*Berengaria, Aquitania, Mauretania*) were scheduled to make a series of four-day 'Cruises to Nowhere.' By cutting down the turn-around periods at New York and Southampton, it was possible to fit these within the regular schedule. Sixteen such trips were listed between April 24 and September 18, at the 'phenomenally' low, all-expense price of $50 up.' Three would be made by the *Berengaria*. The May 15, 1931, *Cunard-Anchor News*, another company paper of the period, had an interesting note about one of the travel agents who sold many tickets on Cunard ships, Fred Lack. 'He keeps right up with the times,' the article said, 'by becoming a tenant of Al Smith in the new Empire State Building. He has the jump on other agents in getting located in the new terminal where Cunard dirigibles will tie up some years hence.' Someone was really thinking ahead.

Despite the hard times, there was always humour. Famed Scott Sir Harry Lauder was invariably called on, when sailing on the *Berengaria*, to be master of ceremonies for fund raisers. On one such occasion he con-

The Berengaria's most famous master, Sir Edgar Britten, photographed on her bridge in December 1932 by Robert L. Coates. Britten was Commodore of the Cunard fleet and would become the first master of the new Queen Mary.

bank. All work on the new Cunard superliner, as yet unnamed, would be stopped. Some 2,500 workers would be laid-off—fired. Appeals for government aid had been rejected. But 1932 would turn out to be slightly better. There would be 14 round trips for the *Berengaria*, instead of 10, and passengers carried transatlantic would total 18,311, instead of 13,408. The new emphasis on Tourist Third Class would be one major factor responsible. 'It's breezy, gay and informal' a new brochure said. 'Frankly, we do not see how anyone with a few hundred dollars and a month or so to spare can hesitate.' Then came what may be the origin of Cunard's famous slogan. It went as follows: 'Going to Europe is only half the pleasure—the other half is travelling on a Cunarder.' And the text continued:

Of course, it's lots of fun. Some people take the viewpoint that a steamship voyage is a necessary evil accompanying a trip to Europe. As soon as they plan to go abroad they begin to sink in the 'slough of despond', over a little matter like a week or so on the briny. Yes, we agree; ocean travel in the early 80s was far from continual ecstasy. Even a quarter of a century ago it would have been difficult to have gone into raptures over the average trans-Atlantic passage—but today things are different.

cluded his efforts by asking whether there were any Scotsmen present. Half a dozen voices shouted: 'Aye-Aye.' Then Sir Harry said: 'Send the hat roond again.'

Great Britain went off the gold standard in September, 1931, an event which had repercussions around the world. Harold P. Borer, general passenger manager for Cunard in America, made the best of this event by announcing: 'Without indulging in prophecy, we sincerely believe that this Fall the American public will recognize more than ever the enduring value of the enhanced purchasing power of the travel dollar.'

On October 14 the *Berengaria* entered the floating dry dock owned by the Southern Railway Co. She would remain there to December 2, and would return from March 11 to April 23 for more work. Things never go quite as planned, though, and the dry dock work was not accomplished as rapidly as had been hoped. She was still there on that gloomy December 11, 1931, long remembered because of a foreboding announcement from the Clyde-

The ship uses Southampton's new floating dry dock in her annual overhaul, a photo taken March 17, 1933. The big two-stacker in the top left at her berth is the Homeric, another ex-German liner. Here also can be seen what the after end of B Deck looked like after the original verandah café was removed for greater stability.

A night view of another Southampton dry-docking. It shows men working around the clock to speed seasonal overhaul. The Associated Press photo had no date. A night scene like this highlights the similarity in outline of Berengaria and Majestic.

The minimum transatlantic fares in First Class on the *Berengaria* were down to only $200 in the summer of 1932. A series of short cruises by Cunard's Big Three was scheduled out of Britain. The *Berengaria*'s would be from Southampton to Madeira. The timing for the ship's second dry-docking had to be set back slightly. A fine night photo was carried in the May, 1932, issue of *Cunard-Anchor News*. Men have been at work day and night to rush the 'rejuvenation' process, the caption said. A new 55-ton rudder was installed, which had been sent from Darlington to Southampton by truck, having been too big to be brought by rail. The truck which brought it had had two drivers, one in front and one in the rear, who had kept in touch by telephone.

Then there was another unexpected setback: a disastrous fire on May 6 destroyed Cunard's Pier 54 on Manhattan. Cunard's Big Three had to move over to Hoboken at this point. Pier 54 was not reopened until early in 1933, and cost Cunard $1,000,000 to restore.

Brochures in foreign languages were a regular thing to lure passengers who were recent arrivals in America, and wished to see what it was like in their old homelands. One was issued on September 6, 1932, in Italian. Featuring Third Class facilities on the *Berengaria*, it described a conducted tour led by Sig. E. Trippitelli.

A new low in passenger lists was the September 29, 1932, departure from New York, with only 134 aboard in all classes. On December 14, 1932, the *Berengaria* left New York as part of a new service linking the US Pacific Coast with India. Only 18 days would be required to carry high grade package freight from San Francisco to Karachi.

The year 1933 finally saw the beginning of the end of the great Depression. Perhaps this might be a good point for more comments from the autobiography of Captain Harry Grattidge, who had served on the *Berengaria*. He summarized his attitude in one sentence—'She was a gleaming and bejewelled ferry boat for the rich and titled.' Probably the choice anecdote in Capt. Gattidge's *Berengaria* memories involves a time in between crossings, when she lay idle and lonely at her pier and the good Captain was her watch officer. There were only six old watchmen aboard. Capt. Grattidge had just completed his rounds and was dozing off when there was a pounding on his door. One of the watchmen, stuttering with excitement, said that the Prince of Wales . . . he paused for breath . . . was in the Ballroom. Capt. Grattidge hurried there and, as he approached, heard sounds of jazz. He found a troop of musicians in evening clothes playing with great gusto. Their leader, baton in hand, was the Prince. Still in the darkened edge of the huge two-deck high saloon, and as yet unnoticed, Grattidge heard the Prince thanking each musician and saying that cheques would be in the post to them by the next morning. As he led the party to the gangplank, Grattidge summoned the nerve to ask the Prince how he had happened to pick the *Berengaria* for his jazz session. The Prince replied: 'It was very convenient, of course, and, well, I thought we shouldn't be disturbed. Sometimes, you know, it is very hard to find a place where you can be alone.'

The *Berengaria* made headlines on November 16, 1933. Six ships had been racing to help the little British freighter *Saxilby*, whose crew of 27 was reported to be abandoning ship in a raging North Atlantic storm. Captain Britten was on the bridge when the call for help came. Changing his course he speeded up to 20 knots. The *Saxilby* was a ship of 3,630 tons out of West Hartlepool, bound for Port Talbot, Wales. She was on the western track some 200 miles away from the *Berengaria*, which was 300 miles west of London homeward bound on the eastern track. Sad to say, the last radio message received from the little freighter was broken off after giving only two letters: 'go . . .' On the *Berengaria*, hoping against hope, Capt. Britten called for lifeboat volunteers. 'In the face of almost certain death,' he said later, 'I am proud to say that every man of my crew offered himself for service.' But all was to no avail. Two hours later, at midnight, with every searchlight ablaze, the *Berengaria* searched the area slowly and in zigzagging circles. She stayed by until dawn. Nothing was ever found of the *Saxilby*.

The year 1934 would be an epochal year for Cunard. For the *Berengaria* it would be the beginning of the end. Passenger traffic on the

Atlantic was up enough to warrant scheduling her for her maximum number of round trips—16. For the full year of 1934 she carried 17,307 across the Atlantic, over 2,500 more than in 1933. The Depression was beginning to fade. Also on the plus side, her master had been knighted. He was now Sir Edgar Britten, or Sir Edgar for short. Scheduling was a decidedly fluid thing in these trying days. The *Berengaria* was listed to sail on January 6 to begin her new year, but as things turned out she did not make her first departure until February 3. The month of January was used for another major overhaul. The cranes in front of her bridge were replaced by king-posts and derricks. John Isherwood states that 'the bulkheads round her fore deck forward of the side-to-side mast house were removed.' Another interesting change was made by painting her lifeboats white. Previously they had been dark, either painted or stained a dark brown. This had always given her a most distinctive, yacht-like look. A major development came on February 8, while the *Berengaria* was in mid

Atlantic. Great Britain made known a policy change aimed at regaining the Blue Riband from Germany. With the financial assistance of 10 Downing Street, the Cunard Line and the White Star Line would be merged. The new company would be called Cunard-White Star, Ltd., and would have a combined fleet of 25 ships, headed by Cunard's *Berengaria* and White Star's *Majestic*. At last, two of the three Albert Ballin 50,000 tonners were together.

'For what is believed to be the first time in the history of the company, the three trans-Atlantic express liners of Cunard Line—*Berengaria*, *Aquitania*, and *Mauretania*—will arrive in New York within the space of four

The Chelsea piers at New York with six major liners. From bottom up: Berengaria, Laconia, Minnetonka, Homeric, Arabic and Regina. The last mentioned would soon be renamed Westernland. At this point she still has the huge display of lifeboats forward and aft of her twin funnels, a design prompted by the Titanic disaster. A July 11, 1924, photo.

*How things have changed in 10 years, a July 1934
view of the same piers with* Berengaria *approaching
Pier 54 to tie up across from the* Majestic *for the
first time following the meger of Cunard and White
Star. Just above are the* Caledonia, Lancastria, Ile de
France, *and* Conte di Savoia.

days.' So began a piece in the March 4, 1934,
New York Herald Tribune. The *Berengaria* was
maintaining the North Atlantic service alone,
with the two other beauties making cruises.
The best news of the year for Cunard was made
public by the *Associated Press* in a story out
of Glasgow dated March 29, 1934: work would
resume on the new Cunarder. Sailing Schedule No. 1 for Cunard White Star listed two of
the Albert Ballin flagships as first and second,
out of a fleet of 31 liners, probably the largest
fleet of great liners ever to serve under one
management in the post first World War
period. The merger became effective on July 1.

The *Majestic* and *Berengaria* were listed
first and second on the combined fleet list in
that order, because the *Majestic* was a little
larger. Rates for both of them were the same.
On September 26 the new Cunard superliner
was launched. The Cunard-Anchor liner *Tus-
cania* was anchored as a floating grandstand
in the Clyde, as close as possible to the hull
of the new '534', which was expected to be
named *Victoria*, according to the *Herald Tribune* of September 2, 1934. As things turned
out she was christened *Queen Mary*.

The Cunard White Star combine experienced serious growing pains. The new
operation lost money from the start, and drastic action was called for. It came in 1935, with
a vengeance. The March 25 Sailing List
showed nothing particularly new, but a hand-
written note on its cover was a shocker:
'Steamer *Olympic* withdrawn.' Then another
sad blow—the April 22 sailing list had more
bad news: the *Mauretania* was missing. She
was to be sold for scrap. Now the combined
Cunard White Star fleet was only 23 ships.

Two great British passenger liners would be
in the fleet on July 16, at Spithead, when King
George V reviewed the British high seas fleet

on the occasion of the Silver Jubilee of his accession. They were the *Berengaria* and the *Homeric*, both built as German passenger liners just before the First World War. Each would be laden with passengers to see the celebration. Then some more bad news. On August 5, 1935, it was made known that Cunard White Star had lost more than $2,000,000 during its first six months of joint operation; the *Mauretania*'s sale for scrap was confirmed.

On September 11 the *Berengaria* left Southampton after another very fast turnaround. The old girl was really being pushed—turnaround took only 13¼ hours this time. A passing at sea of the *Berengaria* and the *Majestic* is recorded, with the former heading west and the latter approaching the Old World. The *Majestic* was two miles on the port beam, drawing abreast. Let Sir Edgar tell it as he saw it: 'As she passes, her flag flutters slowly down from the mast head. That is a compliment to me—she is raising her hat to her Commodore. We return the salute.'

The really bad news came on November 2, 1935, in a special wire story from London. The headlines blared out the story: 'BERENGARIA TO QUIT ATLANTIC IN SPRING. Beginning May 27 when the *Queen Mary* starts her maiden voyage, the *Berengaria* will be laid up and the express service will be operated by the *Queen Mary, Majestic* and *Aquitania*.' The first of the Ballin Big Three's last sailings was May 8. Her name was not shown on Cunard White Star's summer list of sailings.

On November 24 a follow up story appeared in New York papers. It began:

When the Berengaria arrived here last week the crew was eager for the latest reports about the retirement of the ship from service. According to the new sailing schedule the Berengaria *will arrive in New York on May 5 and sail on May 8 for the last time. On arrival in the home port May 14, the crew of 950 officers and men will be transferred to the* Queen Mary, *which is due to sail from Southampton on May 27 and will carry a crew of more than 1,000 all told.*

A final note for the year 1935: on December 15 it was announced that Captain Reginald V. Peel, master of the *Aquitania* and Commodore in the Royal Naval Reserve (Retd.), will leave his ship on her arrival at Southampton and take command of the *Berengaria* in place of Captain Sir Edgar Britten. Sir Edgar would go to the *Queen Mary*.

The new year brought great news for the men and women of the *Berengaria*. A sudden policy shift was announced on January 2, 1936, when she was put into the King George V dry dock at Southampton for her annual overhaul. A report released by Britain's *Planet News* trumpeted: 'The famous ship is to retain her place in the North Atlantic service, the *Majestic* having been condemned to the ship breakers instead.' Of the two merged lines, Cunard obviously was in command.

Freshly painted, with a roistering crew aboard, the *Berengaria* started on her first of 16 westbound crossings in mid January, 1936, reaching New York on January 22 and sailing right on through early October. She would carry a healthy 19,944 passengers on 16 westbound trips and 15 eastbound, slightly down from her 1935 carryings.

On April 1, 1936, three war-orientated steps were taken by Cunard White Star. War clouds had been gathering over Europe for some time, and Hitler's continuously aggressive actions were causing many to be concerned about the future. As April began, Britain's Postmaster-General, Major G.C. Tyron, and British ship line representatives signed a new mail contract which included ominous provisions relating to the distribution of naval intelligence, encouragement of the Royal Naval Reserve movement among the officers and men on board the contractors' ships, and preparation of contracting companies 'at the expense of the Admiralty to carry six-inch guns.' Whether the *Berengaria* was ever fitted with such weapons is not known at this writing.

One interesting ship news story came out of the midsummer voyaging of the *Berengaria*. When she arrived on July 21, 1936 at New York, her First Officer, G.E. Barton, was cornered by a ship news reporter from the *Herald Tribune*, and it was revealed that First Officer Barton was on the bridge when a large

Berengaria *entering King George V drydock, having retained her place in the North Atlantic service when, as Planet News recounted 'the Majestic was condemned to the ship-breakers instead'. The date of the photo and caption was January 2, 1936.*

school of whales was sighted off the starboard bow. They were approaching the ship and Barton was faced with a problem. If he continued on course he would in all probability hit one or more of the huge mammals. If he turned, he would consume more fuel, and company rules said that he should not burn extra fuel without proper justification. He could make a course change to avoid hitting a fishing boat, for example, but what to do about whales? As he told the reporter: 'I was once on the *Homeric* when we rammed a whale. It was an ugly mess, and we had to back off to shake it off,' he said. 'We can't do that on the *Berengaria*, as we are a fast mail ship and can't afford to waste time shaking whales off our bow. It's better to give them leeway and call it square.' So the First Officer ordered the course altered by about two degrees and gave the whales the right of way. 'I may say that they seemed to enjoy the courtesy,' he added. 'One of the big fellows literally leaped out of the water and apparently had no difficulty standing on his tail for a second or so.' By careful manoeuvring, the Chief Officer was able to make up for the delay and so accounted for the slight extra fuel expenditure. He did not consult the ship's master, Captain Peel, who had turned in before the school was sighted. The *Tribune's* reporter had an opportunity to visit briefly with Captain Peel, and learned that Peel would take command of the *Queen Mary* on August 6, so that Sir Edgar Britten could have a brief vacation. 'Don't say I'm relieving the Commodore. I don't like the word "relieve",' Captain Peel said.

Not quite four months later, the brand new Queen Mary *prepares to leave for her trials as* Berengaria *heads out across the Atlantic from her Southampton berth. Note the* Queen Mary *does not have the stem anchor. It would not be until the* Queen Elizabeth *that Cunard naval architects would catch up with their German rivals on this count.*

The first of a long series of fires took place late in 1936 on the *Berengaria*, while she was undergoing an overhaul at Southampton. Several cabins caught fire, for an unknown reason, while she was at the Ocean Dock, where she has been laid up for a fortnight. The blaze was extinguished in half an hour, and only seven or eight cabins were damaged, mostly from water. The fire had been discovered by a crew member on the starboard side of B Deck under the bridge. The alarm had been sounded and three fire engines had gone to work from the quayside, while three tugs sprayed the liner from the waterside. Firemen fighting the flames through portholes had worked in gas masks.

The *Berengaria* made a round trip to New York over New Year's Day, 1938. Immediately on her arrival at Southampton, she was hurried into dry dock to have her 17-ton bow anchor replaced. A widely used photo of this operation is notable, as it shows the new *Queen Mary* in the background. Shortly after her second round trip the bell began to toll her end, but again no one sensed what was happening. Fire broke out aboard her shortly before midnight on February 14, and several of her cabins were damaged. It was extinguished in an hour or so. At New York during the night of March 2-3, 1938, a second fire within three weeks broke out aboard the *Berengaria* just as she was preparing to depart. There were about 140 passengers aboard, most of them asleep in their cabins. The fire began early in the morning in the Social Hall, then called the Cabin Class lounge. An advertisement in local papers stated that the ship would sail one day late, adding that there was choice accommodation available in all classes. Cunard White Star decided to shut off the Cabin Class areas and sail the vessel with all passengers in Tourist and Third, an indication of how bad the damage was. Photographs appeared on the front pages the next day showing the lounge in a state of chaos, with furniture upturned, hoses everywhere and firemen standing around in their gear. News stories described passengers scurrying about in the dark, smoke-clouded decks in night dress. Four fire companies, a fire boat and crew members fought the blaze from 3.30 to 5 am.

Then a series of dramatic developments took place, all behind the scene, but which would in due course mean the end of the *Berengaria*'s active life. Herbert J. Stevens, a member of the staff of the United States Steamboat Inspection Service, was ordered to investigate. His story is worth telling verbatim:

I went on board and introduced myself to the staff captain and told him what my mission was and he took me to the First Class (Cabin) Saloon and that beautiful space was partly burned out—all the furniture, carpets and rugs ruined and soaked with water for three decks down. After seeing the damage that was done there, I told the captain that I would like to take a look at the tourist quarters and he remarked 'We had a fire there also.' And a space in those quarters 100 feet in length and across the width of the ship was burned out. I asked him when that had happened and he said Southampton, this trip. On German ships built during that time electrical circuits had one-way wiring and were grounded to the steel hull and house plates. Over the years, a ship some 900 feet long when entering and leaving the Gulf Stream the expansion and contraction was considerable along with the changes of seasons. With the ship's motion, the wires would slacken and chafe on the steel plates and when the insulation wore off a short circuit occurred and if there is an accumulation of dust, a fire. I told the captain that I did not think his ship was seaworthy for carrying US passengers and would recommend the Treaty Certificate be taken down. Captain George Fried, supervising inspector in our office, asked me to meet him at the gangplank and, if he found the conditions to be as I told him, he would verify my decision. I removed the Treaty Certificate.

Captain Fried was one of the Atlantic's best known skippers having won honours for a number of rescues on United States Lines pas-

senger ships. It was most fortunate that he was in charge. The Cunard White Star were quite unhappy. The *Berengaria*'s master, Captain George Gibbons, announced that the ship had been examined and passed by the Steamboat Inspection Service on her arrival several days before. His statement continued: 'There was a minor fire in the lounge early Thursday morning which involved seepage of water into numerous cabin rooms below this compartment, and this caused the company to decide to exclude cabin passengers on this voyage out of consideration for their comfort.' Following the fire, Lloyd's examined the ship and granted a seaworthy certificate. The vessel was to sail at 11 am. Then word of Captain Fried's action changed everything. By this time about 415 passengers were aboard, including 160 who had paid for First Class travel. About 60 of these decided to transfer to Tourist Class, including Michael MacWhite, Irish Minister to the United States; Lord Dawson of Penn, former physician to King George V, and Lady Dawson, and Martin Van Buren, 82-year-old world traveller. The remaining First Class passengers would remain in New York to await the sailing of the *Queen Mary* the following week.

Newspapers added more details about the blaze. The 40 First Class passengers whose cabins were in the immediate area of the water damage and smoke came on deck with wet handkerchiefs over their faces. Lights on the ships were turned off because it was feared a short circuit may have been the cause of the fire. Fire Department searchlights were set up all along the pier flooding the *Berengaria*'s decks with their beams. Captain Gibbons, who with other officers was in quarters directly forward of the main saloon, directed the fire fighting and maintained order aboard this vessel, despite the clouds of smoke pouring through the First Class cabin windows. Captain Fried was quoted in a terse statement: 'I refused to certificate the *Berengaria* for passengers because I didn't believe she was safe for passengers after my inspection this morning. She has had two fires recently. Go look at the Third Class and I think you'll agree with me. I have nothing more to say.' The *Herald Tribune's* reporter added this from his personal experience: 'A brief visit to the section on F Deck in Third Class of the 26-year-old liner showed that the walls and ceilings of steel were smoke blackened and all the cabin partitions in that section had been ripped out. But the section had been shut off from other accommodations.'

Harold P. Borer, general manager of the Cunard White Star Line, issued the following statement to passengers booked to sail:

The company regrets very much to advise that the Berengaria will not carry any passengers on this sailing. It was, of course, anticipated that the ship would receive clearance from the US authorities and a seaworthy certificate had already been received from Lloyd's representative at New York, following inspection on Thursday. However this morning the US Steamboat Inspection Dept. declined to issue a passenger certificate. In accepting passengers in the tourist and third class, the company was satisfied that it acted in complete accord with its traditional policy of safeguarding its passengers and carrying them in comfort. It was with a view to passengers' comfort alone that it decided not to carry cabin passengers, due to possible seepage of water from the Lounge to the First Class staterooms below. The company is most regretful for the inconvenience that has been caused its passengers.

While passengers were debarking with their baggage and planning to stay at hotels through the courtesy of the line, the company gave a statement to the press duplicating, in most part, the explanation given to passengers. This statement emphasized that the company 'had no alternative but to sail the vessel on this voyage without passengers.' It was added further that the liner carried both cargo and mail. Fifty of her stewards did not sail, and were put ashore to be transferred to the *Queen Mary* to accommodate the overflow of passengers from the *Berengaria*. Mr Borer added that the *Berengaria* was scheduled to make a number of summer and fall cruises from New York between June 1 and October 15, along with other company liners.

One way wiring was common on ships built before the First World War, but it has been outlawed by international safety conventions for

A comparison of B Decks on Imperator and on Vaterland, showing great advantages of the split uptakes, how much more open space was provided. For the first time a central passage was possible on the stateroom decks as well. (Society of Naval Architects & Marine Engineers)

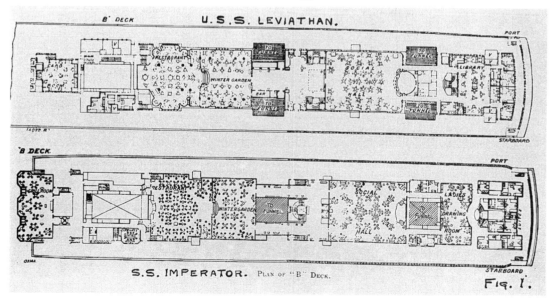

March 31, 1938, was a sad day for Berengaria. Here she is being shifted to No. 108 berth at Southampton, where 'she will lay-up indefinitely' following her withdrawal from Atlantic service after a series of fires. The Olympic, Mauretania and Majestic all were tied up at this spot before being ordered to the scrap yard.

many years, as a serious cause of fires. At this writing, two-way wiring is standard and much safer. Captain Fried's brave action was thoroughly vindicated soon after the *Berengaria* arrived at Southampton, when another fire broke out on March 16. It was quickly extinguished by the ship's crew, and a company statement said that the damage was slight.

On March 21, 1938, Cunard White Star announced that she would be retired, and on October 19 it was made known that she would be sold for scrap. She was towed to Berth 108—the same place where the *Olympic, Mauretania* and *Homeric* had been laid up before being sent to the breakers. On November 7 she was bought for scrap by Sir John Jarvis. He paid £500,000 for her to give work to the Jarrow unemployed. A Member of Parliament, he had for years interested himself in jobless shipyard workers in his area. On December 6 the *Berengaria* left Southampton on her last voyage, to the scrapyard. All shipping in Southampton joined in a mournful salute as the 52,101-ton liner put out to sea. She arrived under her own power, still looking like a queen. A picture in a full-page Anchor Tugs advertisement shows her entering the Tyne with two tugs assisting at her bow.

The scrapping was interrupted by the war, and a large portion of the old ship's double bottom remained throughout the conflict. On July 23, 1946, this remnant was cut in half and the fore-section set out on a final trip, with seven Anchor tugs helping. The tow crossed the Tyne bar two hours later and three large tugs took over. The 'raft', as it was called, arrived the next day at 4.30 pm at the Firth of Forth, where both the *Leviathan* and the *Majestic* had been scrapped. The after section followed, and both segments were soon disposed of. Thus all three of Albert Ballin's Big Three were dismantled on about the same spot.

② LEVIATHAN

〜〜〜

$\mathcal{T}$he *Leviathan* became America's best-known liner during the First World War. She started her spectacular career as the *Vaterland*, second of Hamburg American Line's trio of 50,000-ton passenger liners, and pride of their president — Albert Ballin.

It is quite unusual for someone to write a six-volume work on one subject and follow it with an abbreviated summary, but this is what I am doing here. It has not been easy to condense my original million word tome into a 10,000 word capsule, but there are some advantages. I have been able to put in some delightful anecdotes that I discovered too late for my original effort, and I have been able to use a large number of new photos that I could not find space for in my much larger six volumes, despite its roughly 2,300 oversize pages. About 12,000 volumes of my original study of the *Leviathan* have been sold, leaving an equal number unsold. In other words there are plenty left for you if you do not have a set. I was the publisher and I have the remaining volumes in my cellar. I like to feel that this work will reach many times as many readers as my more expansive effort. I am eager to have new readers understand my passion for this second of Albert Ballin's 'Big Three'. And now permit me to quote a little from my preface

The knife-like bow of Leviathan, *dry docked at South Boston. Note the fresh white boot topping and the stem anchor.* (Morris Rosenfeld)

to Volume I of my series:

Aside from all the exciting moments, the many 'firsts' and the stream of adventure that makes the Vaterland/ Leviathan *story interesting, there is an intangible attraction that has drawn me to her. It is the pathos enshrouding her life. So human, so like a living thing was she, and so transitory, so much a creature of fortune, a setting for contrasts. Even in her great moments, and there were many, she was a target of sarcasm. Even in her days of white-elephant neglect, she was a thing of awe, a loved presence. A creature of mass and beauty, she was an extraordinary entity. Like the Great Pyramid, or Chatres Cathedral she represented much more than the total of her parts. Unlike these architectural masterpieces her span was brief. This perhaps, above all, impels me to attempt to document her short appearance on life's sea.*

Albert Ballin's second 50,000 tonner began life as Hull 212 of Blohm & Voss, Hamburg. Her earliest plans had been drawn up by Harland & Wolff, Belfast, but when Blohm & Voss conceived of a striking new design idea, they got the work, not only for this ship but for the third of the dream trio. The new concept was the idea of split uptakes. Ever since the elegant steam ship *Savannah*, of 1819, all ocean-going steamers had uptakes that carried the smoke from the engines up and out via centre-line funnels. As was only natural, these uptakes were located directly in the middle, or choice part of the ship. It was only natural, something no one ever even thought about. All the public rooms had to be built around these central uptakes. Galleries had to run on either side, they could never run down the middle. This was true for every ocean-going ship built until Hull 212. With split uptakes, however, there were two upward ducts for the smoke to travel by. They were built on either side of the ship and joined on the boat deck under each of the two real funnels. The dummy, of course, had no split uptakes.

The result was an elegance and spaciousness never dreamed of in any ship ever built previously. The ship's main public rooms could be laid out using the very centre of the hull. One huge public room after another, and no need to fit them around the central uptake. Great entrance doors from foyers did not have to be to port or starboard, but could open amidships. The concept was a grand one, but expensive. It was so costly that despite its advantages, few ships have ever had it since. Even the three Cunard Queens were not built to have split uptakes. The great German twins *Bremen* and *Europa* had split uptakes, but the famous Italian near-sisters *Rex* and *Conte di Savoia* did not. Even the great *United States* did not benefit from split uptakes.

The *Vaterland*'s hull was formed by 316 frames or ribs, each seven decks high, and numbered from bow to stern. Up to frame 25 the separation was 680 millimetres. The widest spacing was between frames 31 to 291, and this was 915 millimetres. A striking phrase found in one of the *Vaterland*'s printed books of specifications noted that her masts 'are not to be adapted to carry sails.' Although the *Savannah* had made her famous Atlantic crossing using steam power in 1819, it was not until the 1880s that fast liners with twin propellers could feel safe in abandoning sails. Sails were carried on many steamships as late as 1914.

The three 64-foot funnels of Hull 212 were each supported by 16 guy wires. Eight were anchored at the first rib half way up, and eight more at the second, two-thirds of the way to the top. Had these ribs been used, when the ship became the *Leviathan*, as the marking points dividing the red, white and blue painted areas, the ship would have looked much finer. This is how the artist's conception by Worden Wood showed the funnels. They were huge, measuring 30 feet in length and 20 feet in width. Another special feature of the *Vaterland* was her bridge front. I believe it was an improvement over the very fine forward-facing superstructure of the *Imperator*. A sense of height and massiveness was created by two wide columns resting on the forward end of the Promenade Deck (B Deck). The bridge proper jutted out six feet on either side giving the ship a maximum beam of 112 feet. The bridge and the Pilot House were stained mahogany, an improvement over the white-painted steel of the *Imperator*. And the monkey bridge atop the Pilot House was white, framing the stained bridge proper. The bridge was not square, but slanted out at either end, giving a sculptured feeling of elegance. Below the bridge was the deck-and-a-half-high forward face of the Smoking Room, recessed to provide a walkway around the forward end of the Boat Deck. The bulkhead for this walk-around was also stained mahogany. Four white steel struts rose up from this bulkhead, giving obvious support to the bridge and permitting a fine view from the deck-and-a-half-high windows, broken into sections by three horizontal and one vertical dividers. Another row of windows running across the bridge front gave protection to the forward end of the Promenade. The two lower decks had portholes facing forward. Although the *Bismarck*'s bridge front was identical, it never had the éclat that the *Vaterland*'s had, probably because the pilot house and Boat Deck bulkheads were not stained mahogany.

Hull No. 212 would be 950 feet overall, and the ship would measure 54,000 gross tons. She would have 83 lifeboats, each with sails, and two would also be engine powered. There would be 5,500 life jackets. Every phase of the building saw new techniques used. The three million rivets, weighing five pounds each, were to be driven home by the latest hydraulic device, twice man-sized. The ship's double bottom was five and a half feet wide.

Ballin dropped his original plan to name Hull 212 *Europa* when he learned that the Kaiser wanted to make political capital out of naming her *Vaterland*. The Kaiser was trying to bring the old Kingdom of Bavaria closer into the German confederation. He asked Ballin to invite King Ludwig of Bavaria to christen the ship, thinking this would be a way the latter could comfortably be drawn into the larger Germany concept. As it happened Ludwig, who had at first accepted, would ask his son Prince Rupprecht to take his place as the ship's sponsor. The launching took place on April 3, 1913. Moments before the ceremonies, Hermann Blohm and Ernst Voss escorted Prince Rupprecht around the great hull, with Albert Ballin a few paces behind. Ballin had a happy smile on his face. It was undoubtedly the greatest moment of his life.

Despite his worries about a foreboding war and his deep unhappiness over the Kaiserin's prejudices against him, he was having a wonderful time and was devoting all his energies to making the *Vaterland* the finest ship that had ever existed, in every way. His choice of Blohm & Voss had been a good one and the *Vaterland* gave every promise of being even more luxurious than the wonderful *Imperator*. Everything aboard—from the delicately formed letter 'V' interwoven into the decorative glass frame over the double doors leading aft out of the great Social Hall into the B Deck main foyer, to the four huge oil paintings presented to the ship by the Kaiser— every inch of the vast ship was his personal field of battle, of triumph. The great oils would survive to the end of the ship's relatively short career, only to be sold and destroyed in a fire at a British seaside resort. They measured 12 by 13 feet, without their massive frames. Painted in the late 17th Century by the Flemish artist Gerard de Lairesse, they depicted the Pandora myth. The Kaiser also contributed a priceless bronze of Marie Antoinette, created

in 1780 by the famous French sculptor Houdon. The Smoking Room had walls of tooled leather and elaborate wood carving. Four 27-inch oak statuettes of seamen, known as the 'Old Salts', were part of this exquisite detail, each supporting columns bracketing entranceways to elegant alcoves. Within each alcove were leaded-glass windows with stained glass inserts depicting the different kingdoms and duchies of old Germany.

Great care was taken with passenger accommodation. All bedsteads in First Class were of brass and each cabin had a marble washstand with hot and cold water, front and side mirrors, sockets for electric plugs, and even a built-in flower holder. Some 136 cabins had private bath and toilet or shower. The average size of a double cabin was 172 square feet, while the two Imperial Suites each covered 247 square feet, each boasting nine rooms, including a private verandah. The legend on the deck plans of this fabulous ship featured an abbreviation neither used before nor since on any other ship deck plan, as far as I know: the letters 'FP' which indicated a stateroom with a fireplace. With every cabin filled, the *Vaterland* could carry 4,050 passengers. She came closer to reaching this top capacity with a 1929 crossing, on which over 2,700 passengers were aboard, more than any other ship of the interwar era. She had a crew of 1,200 and a lifeboat capacity of 5,300. Her crew, it should be mentioned, remained at this high original figure in later years, although the crew of the *Imperator/Berengaria* dropped to just over 800 and that of the *Bismarck/Majestic* was cut to about 900.

The *Vaterland* was drawing 37 feet when she began her passage down the Elbe on April 25, 1914. Many thousands watched. Shipyard workers on the partly finished *Cap Polonia*, the three-funnelled beauty being built for Hamburg South American Line, waved. Twice on the way down, the new sea queen paused to avoid running aground. On both occasions she was passed by a four-masted barque named *Valkyrie*, whose crew cheered each time, none with more vigor than a young seaman named Charles Rosner. He was to become one of America's best known marine artists. The Blohm & Voss trials were run on April 29 and

In the North Sea on her trials — the Vaterland.

30, and to everyone's delight the ship achieved a speed of 26.3 knots, developing 90,400 shaft horsepower. The transatlantic record was 26.06 knots, held by the sleek Cunarder *Maureta-nia*. Commodore Ruser, however, refused to even hint that a speed record would be attempted on the maiden voyage. A second set of trials, with Prince Franz of Bavaria aboard, were held on May 10 for Hapag. Then back to Cuxhaven for the final preparations. The first crossing would begin at 2 pm on Thursday, May 14, 1914.

Passengers had begun boarding at mid morning, and by noon luncheon was being served in all of the four large dining saloons. Only about 1,000 were booked from Cuxhaven, with another 600 to join at Southampton or Cherbourg. The 58-page passenger list included advertisements for flights on the company dirigible, *Hansa*. Four directors of Hapag were aboard, all in high spirits because the *Vaterland* had beaten the Cunarder *Aquitania* into service. Sixteen Americans among the Cuxhaven passengers may have chuckled at the English translation of the handsome 76-page booklet—'Handbook for Passengers'—with its red, white and black tassel. Some of the word-

ing was a bit Teutonic, such as: 'Passengers will please inform their room steward regarding the manner in which they wish to have made up their beds.'

A tremendous German flag flattened in the breeze from its staff at the stern when the ship reached Cowes. The red and gold castle flag of Hamburg whipped in the wind forward, and 15 brand new code flags snapped this way and that from the fore and main masts. In no time the great, glistening, grand new beauty was off and headed toward Cherbourg. The weather was calm as the *Vaterland* passed the lightship off the Isle of Wight and headed toward the French coast. It was a beautiful early summer day. Then one of those delightful coincidences—into sight came the little American liner *St. Louis*, in her 20th year and tiny by comparison. On her bridge was her First Mate—Herbert Hartley and her master, John Clark Jamison. Each were to serve as master aboard the huge liner when she came to be known as the *Leviathan*. But neither could have dreamed this possible by the wildest stretch of their imagination at that moment. Hartley spoke: 'Sir, the captain of that ship must indeed be a proud man.' To this old Captain Jamison replied: 'Let him try to get up the English Channel some dirty night when he doesn't know where he is and he

Deck scene on a 1914 Vaterland crossing. First Class passengers relax in their deck chairs. The lady at the far right does not seem too relaxed, though, does she?

Happy faces on the Boat Deck, as deck games draw a large crowd aboard the Vaterland.

Promenading on the Vaterland's *glass-enclosed Promenade Deck, port side, forward.*

Children in Second Class enjoy the deck too.

Having the boats on D Deck left half the after portion of the Boat Deck proper open for use by First Class passengers — as shown here.

Steerage had a little deck space forward in the well deck.

The Steerage Dining Saloon was neat but not fancy.

The Steerage Pantry. Food in Steerage was plentiful and excellent.

won't feel so damn proud.'

As the new ship left the Channel and headed for America a few hours later, the weather got worse. Steward Fred Hecker lay in an agony of seasickness in his bunk. He had been sick almost continuously on the *Imperator*, but he still loved the sea. He hated to hear all the talk of war between his country and England. Young Zelda Danielevitz, from Gozovo, Russia, had never seen so much food in her life. Her mother had given her a large supply of *zwieback* just in case. She was under 13, but had given her age as 17 so she could travel alone. She used a berth in one of the large cabins for women on J Deck.

The welcome at New York was led by a small 16-foot steamboat built and run by John A. Nernoff. Her shrill scream of a whistle drew a booming reply. Sad to say, the docking at her Hoboken pier was marred by the passing just ahead of a small barge under tow. The gigantic *Vaterland* had to come to a stop and back away. She was caught by river cur-

rents and it took a fleet of over 25 tugs to get her back under control and into the slip. Then on sailing day something happened to her reverse turbine, and she ploughed stern first across the narrow Hudson, causing havoc among small ships and barges on the Manhattan side. She made three round trips and one additional westbound crossing before the war came. She was in New York on August 1, the day the conflict (so pointless and evil in its every connotation) began. Hapag decided to keep her in New York. No one in either Germany or England thought the war would last very long; their blissful ignorance would soon be shattered. Some of the *Vaterland*'s crew went home. Others left the ship and became American citizens. Commodore Ruser's wife joined him and they eventually settled in Morristown, New Jersey.

For the first part of the almost three-year internment, the Germans from the *Vaterland* and the many other interned German liners in Hoboken were treated as visiting guests from a foreign land. Hoboken society was German-orientated. Dances were held aboard the *Vaterland*, to which the cream of society was invited. There were benefits to raise money for bandages and care of German children who had been maimed by British and French bomber attacks on German cities. The atmosphere reflected the confused state of the American mind—which side should the United States back? Then all changed; instead of friends, the Germans became spies and saboteurs, evil conspirators. The sinking of the *Lusitania* did much to bring this drastic alteration in public opinion. And then in April, 1917, led by the Bible-minded philosopher Woodrow Wilson, who 'had kept us out of war', the United States decided to enter the 'war to end all wars'. Ballin's worst possible fears had been realized. Brother had been put against brother. All hopes he had had that his ships would hasten a better understanding between peoples were dashed. His part in the story was over.

As part of the American war hysteria, the myth was spread that the engines of the *Vaterland* were damaged to prevent her use by the United States. This happened on other German ships, but not on the *Vaterland*. On the day of the seizure the *New York Times* noted that the *Vaterland*'s engines were found undamaged. Captain Earl P. Jessop, US engineering officer of the Brooklyn Navy Yard, who was put in charge of the *Vaterland*'s engine overhaul, said there was evidence of poor handling in peacetime, but virtually no malicious damage. Sad to say, the desecration aboard the great ship that followed the US seizure was wanton. Commodore John Baylis, who was in charge of the party that took over the *Vaterland* said: 'It was outrageous. Her US Navy officers and men simply looted her, taking anything and everything. It was so awful that I never forgot it, and when in the Second World War I was captain of the port and had to seize the *Normandie*, I made darn sure it didn't happen again.'

President Wilson asked his wife to suggest a name for the huge ship. She struggled for several days and then returned to him saying: 'I simply can not think of a name.' Without even looking up, the President replied: 'Why, my dear, it is right here in the Bible . . . Leviathan, monster of the deep.' In the years to follow, the great ship would have several

nicknames. Many called her the 'Levi Nathan'. Others knew her as 'The Big Train.' She rapidly became the most famous ship ever to fly the American flag.

The crewing of the *Leviathan* and the training of men to operate her was a massive task done well. She had been more than two years and eight months in the mud at Hoboken when the order for her to move away for engine trials was given. Captain Allan C. Hosell, the undocking pilot, knew that at least 27 feet of silt surrounded her hull. As he ordered slow reverse he felt a sensation of life penetrating even the most remote crevices of the ship. Forty-six tugs helped. Slowly the giantess began to move. A white bloom of steam burst silently and was followed by a blast from her reverse whistle on funnel number 3. It was thunderous and shook the bar fronts up and down River Street.

Dozens of booklets were prepared about how to do things on the USS *Vaterland*, as she was at first called. They were explicit down to the finest detail. The Abandon Ship manual carefully instructed Army officers not to wear spurs during Abandon Ship drills. A few instructions might be highlighted: 'Men vomiting on deck should be made to clean it up.' 'Woodwork must be protected from abuse such as cutting of initials.' 'It is found that a greater morbidity rate exists among troops occupying lower bunks than among those in upper tiers. Much of this is due to dissemination of dust, dried sputum, etc . . .'. The Navy guard was to use the 'utmost courtesy' when calling the attention of any Army officers to infractions of the rules. 'Men in the brig were to bathe and shave on Tuesdays and Fridays.'

Despite all this preparation there was a strong sentiment that the *Leviathan* should not be used as a troopship. Admiral William S. Sims, who was in England in charge of organizing the movement of troops to the war front, spoke out on the subject. She was too big a target for German submarines, he warned. But preparations continued. Captain J.W. Oman was named her master. As there was no dry dock in America large enough to handle her, no one could see what her bottom was like. No true inclining experiments or stability tests could be conducted, and it was decided to limit her initial troop lift to 7,500 men, 500 naval officers and a crew of 1,500. She would be dry-docked in the famous Gladstone Dock at Liverpool. She sailed on Friday, December 14, 1917. Very soon she would put to rest all the worries about her safety as a transport.

The dry-docking at Liverpool was a perilous operation. Piano wires and sighting battens were placed on different decks throughout the ship, designed to detect even the slightest sagging. Massive wooden blocks had been put on the floor of the dock where it was thought they would be most needed. Everything worked. The pumping out of the water took three days. The ship was dry-docked for 27 days, a most difficult period for her huge crew, as no toilet facilities could be used aboard.

J. J. Callahan, one of the Navy crew, nearly bit the top off a ginger ale bottle one day when a barrage of 16 depth charges went off. It was June, 1918, and a periscope had been seen to starboard, or so some thought. That evening Chaplain Eugene E. McDonald, of Sea Cliff, N.Y., had an attentive audience as he read his evening prayer over the loud speaker from the bridge.

Every chunk of coal had to be picked up by hand, put into a basket and lifted aboard from the antiquated French lighters and barges alongside when the *Leviathan* coaled at Brest, which became her French port. With rare exceptions, every crew member had to put in time at this hated detail. Bands played continuously on both sides of the ship all through the night. It took two days to get the 7,800 tons aboard at each visit. A programme of singing was started, with megaphones carrying the voices from the coal barges to the innermost passages of the ship, while the soot-caked men laboured.

Leroy Blackwood, seaman second class, should have been given the prize for tall-tales. After his return home in July he told a New Jersey reporter that the *Leviathan* had survived an 18-hour running fight with U-boats, of which five were sunk. He claimed to have been responsible for sinking three of them 'and a torpedo.' He was wounded slightly from shell splinters. In truth no documented instance of any attack was recorded in the ship's log for

Father E. McDonald, Chaplain on Leviathan. (Dr Georges Schoelles, Sea Cliff)

her period as a troopship, although the Germans claimed on several occasions to have sunk her. The *Leviathan* was well armed, however, and the guns, large and small, were frequently tested. On one such occasion a Quartermaster was standing by a drinking fountain (known as the scuttlebut on shipboard) chatting. A bullet fragment from some gun being tried out ricocheted and hit him on the mouth. The wound gave him a minor but permanent change in his way of talking, something that would later help him a lot in his acting career as a 'tough guy'. His name was Humphrey Bogart.

The September 21, 1918, crossing was awful. Many of the 11,809 men put aboard already had flu. It was an epidemic. Before France was

A part of the huge Navy crew of USS Leviathan, posed on her forward deck. Photo taken July 14, 1919.

No caption has survived with this fine photo. It shows the staff of one of the Leviathan's several daily newspapers printed aboard while she was a troopship. They are standing outside the Printing Office on A Deck. (Lincoln Hedlander)

reached 96 had died, and hundreds of others died later in Brest. Because of a Navy rule that anyone who passed away had to have an autopsy, the dead were piled up in rows on tables on the Promenade deck. They were naked, their entrails piled on their chests, big toes tied together with string, and another piece of string around each penis. Out of this crisis came another 'first' for the *Leviathan*. Navy nurses at sea, something that had never happened before. Mary M. Robinson, Chief Nurse, and Mary Agnes O'Neill, were ordered aboard. 'We were the first nurses assigned to sea duty with the Navy. We were told that whether other nurses were sent would depend on how well we were accepted,' Mary Robinson remembered.

On March 25 and 26, 1919, the largest number of persons ever to sail on one ship came aboard the *Leviathan*—14,416. The war was

Eager to come ashore — returning doughboys and gobs crowd every vantage point as the ship prepares to debark her 14,000 veterans. (Paul Thompson)

Private T.A. Jones in captured German helmet, with another private holding his souvenir rifle, after returning on the Leviathan. *Photo taken December 16, 1918.* (Lincoln Hedlander)

Returning for more troops, with her new camouflage painted on while she was at Liverpool. The Leviathan *is shown approaching her Hoboken pier.*

Her camouflage was different on the port side, as this view shows. The Leviathan was so big that troops had to be ferried ashore in tenders at Brest. (Marcus P. Iverson)

Her rusty greyness is her badge of honour, as she triumphantly brings home 14,000 troops. The whipping out flag at her mainmast, the streamers of sooty grey smoke from her funnels, the puffing exuberance of steam and smoke from the many tugs all make a glamorous halo around the heroic 'Big Train'. (Lincoln Hedlander)

over and the great rush to get home was under way. Secretary of War Newton D. Baker hailed the *Leviathan* as 'the glory of your transport service', adding that her story 'is a romance'. He went on: 'Where shall we find such a tale of co-operation, efficiency and daring? It is a great career, worthy of the greatest ship in the world.' With this was born the phrase used repeatedly by United States Lines, and as the sub-title of my six-volume series on the *Leviathan* ... 'the greatest ship in the world'.

Again on April 7, she took 14,000 home, this time including a young general named Douglas MacArthur, who made enemies of the majority of the returning doughboys by ordering the confiscation of all their German souvenirs, such as helmets. His polished-hat mentality was well developed, even then.

On Tuesday, May 13, 1919, the *Leviathan* arrived at Brest to find the USS *Imperator*, first of Ballin's Big Three, at anchor. There would be a race home. The *Imperator* sailed at 10.30 am, May 15, and was followed by the *Leviathan* 11 hours later. On the 17th she caught up and passed the *Imperator*. The two great liners docked one after the other the following Tuesday.

Frank Tooker, a Naval Reserve cadet, had a glorious time on the ship's penultimate troop-

ing voyage home. He ate in the Officers' mess—'a large and beautiful room'. The breakfast menu, he reported, included steaks and chops. At night he danced with Red Cross girls. He had a stateroom with real beds whose linen was changed daily. He had his own private bathroom with an 'insert electric wall heater.'

General John J. Pershing was aboard on the *Leviathan*'s last crossing as a troopship, along with 100 specially-selected Marines, an honour guard picked because of their height. Over 6,000 radio messages were sent during the crossing. Another 1,000 remained to be transmitted when the radio office finally closed after the ship docked on September 8, 1919. It was another massive welcome, as all the home arrivals had been, with flotillas of tooting craft, flying machines and crowded ferryboats, not to mention salvoes from Fort Wadsworth and sirens blasting everywhere.

Late in 1919 the Shipping Board signed an agreement with the International Mercantile Marine stating that their American Line would be given the task of operating the *Leviathan* on behalf of the US Government. The IMM was also named as the Board's agent in the restoration of the ship to passenger liner status.

William Francis Gibbs, who had so impressed J.P. Morgan before the war when IMM had authorized him to start designing the first 1,000 foot Atlantic liner, held the post of chief of construction and design for IMM. He undertook the creation of a set of blueprints for rebuilding her. He was a self-taught naval architect and marine engineer, and he knew his business. He assembled some hundred draughtsmen, dressed them in spotless white overalls, gave them a pep talk, donned his own overalls and paraded them aboard. The task was on a par with one of the mythical twelve great labours of Hercules. It took nearly two years.

A September 27, 1920, article in the *New York Tribune* summed up the situation with the Ballin Big Three as of that moment in history. Cunard Line was unhappy with the *Imperator*, and would be glad to part with her. The *Bismarck*, still unfinished, was available to the highest bidder. The *Leviathan*, already being called a white elephant, was sitting idle at Hoboken, her future very uncertain. A month later a story in the *New York Times* suggested that she be towed up the Hudson and rebuilt as a floating apartment house—she could be a home for 3,000 homeless. Each such news feature made page one. One rumour after another was given world-wide attention. Even

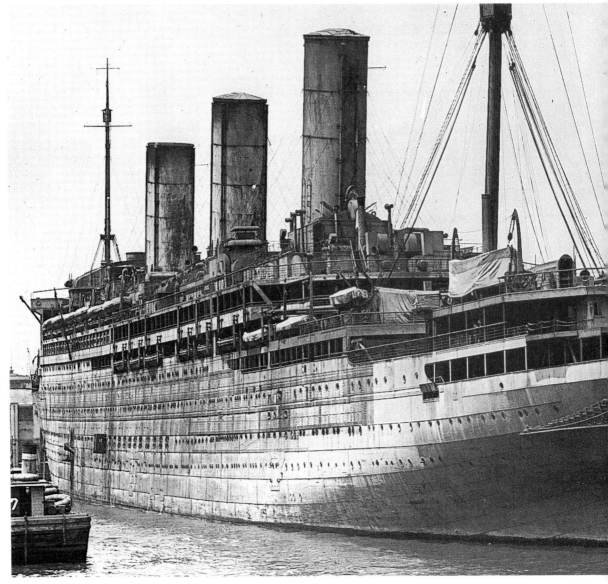

Three great ex-German liners side-by-side at Hoboken. From left to right: Amerika, Leviathan *and* Imperator.

the most preposterous yarns made headlines. There was the tale of how the *Leviathan*'s rat population had multiplied into legions. Fumigation was said to be impractical. Starvation tactics were tried and failed. The *New York World* joked on November 29 that 'the rats on the former German liner had turned Bolshevik and were eating armies of combat cats alive.' A Japanese ship-lover carried the tale home with him, enlarging it in the process. He declaimed: 'Cat troops sent aboard to expel the vast hordes of rampant rodents were met by giant rats of nearly one foot in length who counterattacked and expelled the onslaughting cats.' Then things began to change.

By midyear 1921 the *Imperator* and the *Bismarck* had been acquired, with massive help from the British government, and were being proudly advertised by Cunard and White Star lines. They had been sold to these lines at one-fifth their replacement cost. Their remaining careers roughly paralleled that of the *Leviathan* in point of time, but there the comparison ends. Whereas the next two decades would be years of relatively placid and dignified success for the first and third of Ballin's magnificent trio, they would be tumultuous, heartbreaking and yet glorious years for the *Leviathan*.

William Francis Gibbs had saved the *Leviathan* in 1920. He would win a new ally in the latter half of 1921, a man who would find the way to let Gibbs loose with his dream to rebuild the *Leviathan* and make her truly 'the world's greatest ship.' He was a 41-year-old, six-foot dynamo who had made 'Quaker Oats' a household name. Albert D. Lasker established himself when he was publicity manager for a sick Republican Party and parleyed this post into victory for Warren G. Harding as

With canvas caps over No. two and No. three funnels and her vast array of rubber rafts gone from her sides, the Leviathan *sits idly at Hoboken, beginning her second three-year lay-up here. No one knew what to do with her, she was so big.*

This is how the Leviathan *should have looked had the funnels been painted the way the guy wire ribs suggested. Instead, the white and blue bands were made much smaller. This artist's conception is by Worden Wood, famed US Shipping Board artist. He painted this in 1923 before the ship came out in her US Lines colours. He showed the funnels as being about 50 per cent wider than they actually were, as all artists usually did. Naval architects took some time to catch up to the style suggestions offered in this way by maritime artists, but eventually did, as witness the* Empress of Britain, *and* Normandie.

Photographed April 10, 1922, as reconversion begins at Newport News, Va., the Leviathan *still looks pretty drab.*

President of the United States. In reward he was made Chairman of the US Shipping Board. Lasker not only forced through Washington an agreement to provide the money Gibbs needed to properly restore the *Leviathan*, he also would eventually create a new company to operate her for the government: United States Lines.

William Randolph Hearst, owner of a chain

An artist's conception of Vaterland, *a magnificent bow-on view. This splendid painting was used on the cover of a Hapag brochure printed in 1914. (Norman Brouwer, South Street Seaport Museum)*

Painters leaving the ship May 11, 1922. Note how William Francis Gibbs lettered in the deck designations above the forward sideport. He missed nothing that would speed the work.

of powerful newspapers, and violently anti-British, objected to IMM operating the *Leviathan*. He charged that Morgan's combine included some British-flag ships which were subject to potential control by the British Navy. He won a taxpayers' suit against IMM and on February 16, 1922, the combine announced that it would release the Board from its obligation of allocating the ship to them. This meant that the *Leviathan* would be operated as a single ship by a new and untried company, without any network of trained agents and ticket sellers. All the advantages were on the side of White Star and Cunard, with the two other ships of the Ballin Trio. The Hearst interference put Gibbs on the spot. His passion to rebuild the *Leviathan* now ran counter to the interests of IMM. He was forced to leave the combine and form his own company, Gibbs

Bros. The Shipping Board directed him to complete the restoration. Early in the same year the Newport News Shipbuilding and Day Dock Co., of Newport News, Va., won the contract to rebuild the *Leviathan*. My entire Volume II is devoted to this tremendous task. It tells in detail how Gibbs managed to raise the ship's gross tonnage so she could again claim to be the world's largest, and how he tried to make it appear that she was also the world's fastest. He was so deeply involved that the Shipping Board actually asked him to operate the ship for her first six crossings as an express liner, something that he proceeded to do with relish and gusto. For the rest of her life Gibbs tried to buy her, never succeeding, however.

My own interest in the *Leviathan* was first evidenced by a sketch I did in 1923, the year she returned to peacetime service. I knew how to draw and spell *Leviathan*, but I misspelled my own name when signing my sketch. From her maiden departure on July 4, 1923, the liner continually made headlines. A perfect example was the time she was denounced by Represen-

A stern view taken seven months later, December 6, 1922.

A full broadside, and what a difference, March 21, 1923.

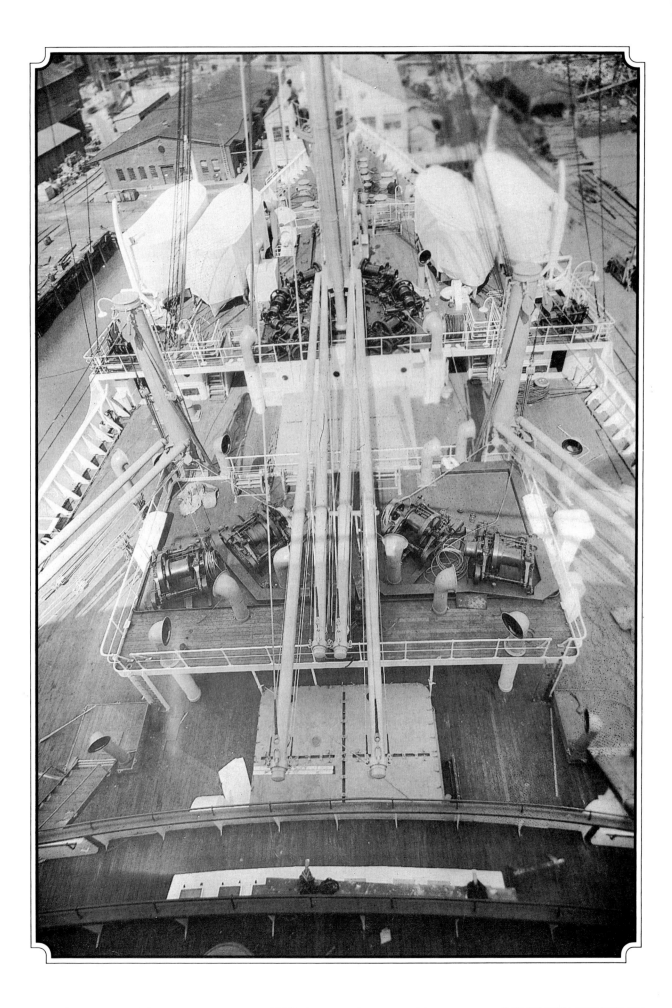

Looking forward from atop the bridge, April 3, 1923

Reconversion work in balcony over First Class Dining Saloon.

First Class Galley looking to port.

Racks, glass and chinaware.

The steering gear is back in shape and ready.

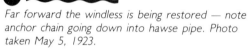

Far forward the windless is being restored — note anchor chain going down into hawse pipe. Photo taken May 5, 1923.

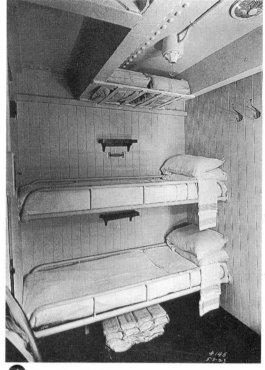

A steerage cabin, clean, neat and ready to serve, on May 3, 1923. Two days later, First Class cabin C168 (below) was also photographed.

 *First Class Smoking Room with Captain Hartley (left foreground). Note the two 'Old Salts' on either side of alcove entrance.*

 *First Class Dining Saloon.*

The Winter Garden, as restored.

Looking from the Palm Court into the Ritz Carlton Restaurant.

The Social Hall, with two of the four Pandora paintings, dating back to the seventeenth century.

BERENGARIA

A Walter Thomas rendering of the Berengaria used by Cunard as a brochure cover in 1923.

A 1932 week-end cruise brochure with price 'reduced' to $40 for the five-day trip.

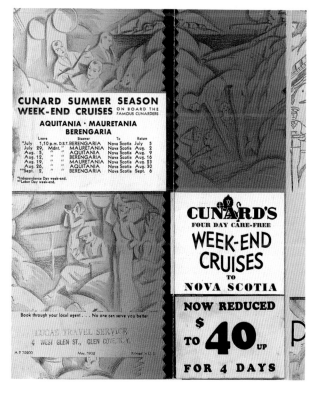

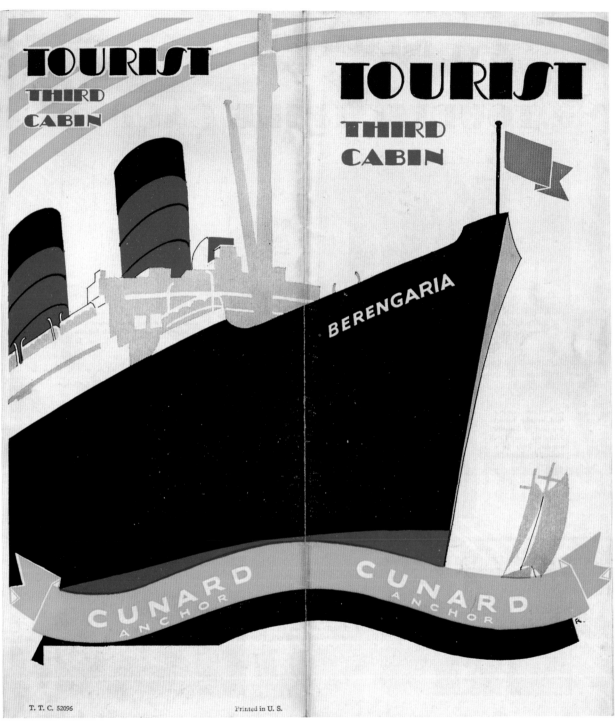

THIRD
CABIN

TOURIST
THIRD
CABIN

BERENGARIA

CUNARD
ANCHOR

CUNARD
ANCHOR

T. T. C. 52096 Printed in U. S.

An art deco brochure for Tourist Third Cabin on the Berengaria.

A breakfast menu in First Class. (Richard Keller)

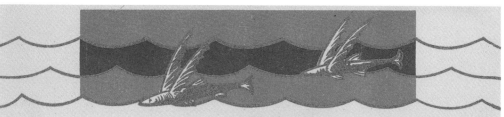

Cunard
White Star

R.M.S. BERENGARIA   SATURDAY, JULY 25, 1936

BREAKFAST

*   *   *   *

FRUITS

Grape Fruit   Oranges   Plums   Pears   Cherries   Water Melon

Honey Dew Melon   Pineapple   California Figs in Syrup

Baked Apples   Compote of Prunes and Figs

ICED JUICES—Sauerkraut   Tomato   Orange   Pineapple

CEREALS

Oatmeal Porridge   Cream of Wheat

Quaker Oats   Plasmon Oats   H. O. Oats   Bonny Boy Toasted Oats

Grape Nuts   Bemax   Breakfast Bran   Force Whole Wheat (Flakes)

Shredded Wheat   Post Toasties   Corn Flakes   Post's Bran Flakes

TO ORDER (10 mins.) : Soupe à l'Oignon Gratinée

FISH

Grilled Pickerel—Maitre d'Hôtel   Fried Yellow Perch   Salt Mackerel, Parsley Sauce

Yarmouth Bloaters   Salmon Fish Cakes

EGGS—Fried, Turned, Boiled, Shirred, Poached and Scrambled

OMELETTES—Spanish, Lyonnaise, Mushrooms, and Tomato—to order

ENTREES

Calf's Brain Fritters   Roast Beef Hash   Hashed Turkey au Gratin

GRILL

American, Wiltshire and Irish Pale Bacon   Canadian, York and Danish Ham

Devilled Mutton Bones   Minute Steak   Sheep's Kidneys—Vert-Pré

Halstead Sausages

Potatoes—Mashed, Sautè, Hashed Brown

French Fried

COLD MEATS ASSORTED

Radishes   Spring Onions   Cucumber   Watercress   Mustard and Cress

CAKES

Griddle and Buckwheat Cakes—Maple Syrup   Waffles   Scotch Oat Cake

VARIOUS BREADS

White Rolls   Graham Rolls   Energen Rolls   Hovis Bread   French Toast

Currant Bread   Sultana Bread   Toasted Muffins   Sultana Scones   Soda Scones

French Crescents   Cottage Loaves   Vienna Bread   Cinnamon Buns

Preserves—Strawberry   Raspberry   Plum   Black Currant   Damson

Grape Fruit Marmalade   Greengage   Apricot   Orange Marmalade   Honey   Guava Jelly

Tea—Indian, Ceylon and China   French Coffee   Instant Postum   Kaffee Hag Coffee   Cocoa

Cadbury's Cup Chocolate   Buttermilk   Ovaltine

Horlick's Malted Milk—Plain and Chocolate

Fleischman's Yeast Cakes

Passengers on Special Diet are especially invited
to make known their requirements to the Head Waiter

CUNARD LINE   R M S "BERENGARIA"   TONNAGE 52,300

A splendid artist's conception of the Berengaria, *used on a Cunard postcard.* (Richard Keller)

Another postcard rendering, both printed in England.

CUNARD LINE   R.M.S. "BERENGARIA"   TONNAGE 52,300

An interesting stern view used as a colour postcard.

*A pre-*Queen Mary *period postcard of* Berengaria, *in the art deco style.*

LEVIATHAN

Brochure cover, circa 1928, with crowds waving;
printed when the Leviathan was government-owned.

A poster by R.S. Pike; while tremendously
exaggerated, it was ideal for its purpose. The blue
and white bands on the stacks are much wider than
they actually were. The wording that was a part of
this poster is missing.

S.S. LEVIATHAN
UNITED STATES LINES

My Travels Abroad

WardBound Quality

MADE IN U. S. A.

A 1923 menu cover, featuring a painting by C. Haye. The menu was for Dinner, August 23, 1923.

The title page shown here features the Wordon Wood painting of the Leviathan, with wide white and blue bands, as he would have preferred to have seen them.

Playing cards used on the Leviathan. They featured an eagle design by William Francis Gibbs.

One of the famous Tuck company postcards of Leviathan.

A Leviathan postcard published by J. Salmon, Ltd., in England.

A postcard, dating from the time the IMM owned the Leviathan. The slogan on the back no longer read 'world's greatest ship', but was toned down to 'America's greatest ship'.

S.S. "LEVIATHAN"
(UNITED STATES LINES) AT CHERBOURG.

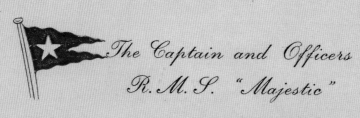

The Captain and Officers
R.M.S. "Majestic"

AT HOME

Thursday, December Fifth,

ONE THOUSAND NINE HUNDRED AND TWENTY-NINE,

request the pleasure of

▬▬▬▬▬▬▬▬▬ *presence*

Reception 8 p.m.
Dancing 8.30 p.m. to 1 a.m.

R.S.V.P.
Officers' Quarters,
Pier 59, North River.

PLEASE PRESENT INVITATION CARD AT GANGWAY.

R·M·S
MAJESTIC
56,621 TONS
The World's Largest Liner

★ ★ ★

WHITE STAR LINE

MAJESTIC

An invitation to a reception aboard the Majestic on December 5, 1929. There would be dancing in the 'officers' quarters'.

The cover of a brochure featuring the Majestic's sumptuous interiors.

Eight children were invited to this party on November 7, 1932: Charles Baker, James Bayliss, Sara Costa, Robert Dynes, Herbert Lorenzon, Edna Patrick, George Whitfield and Terence Vickers.

A postcard painting by Montague Black in 1922.

Children's Tea Party.

R.M.S. "MAJESTIC"

White Star Line

WHITE STAR LINE.

QUADRUPLE-SCREW R.M.S. "MAJESTIC,"
56,551 TONS.
THE LARGEST STEAMER IN THE WORLD.

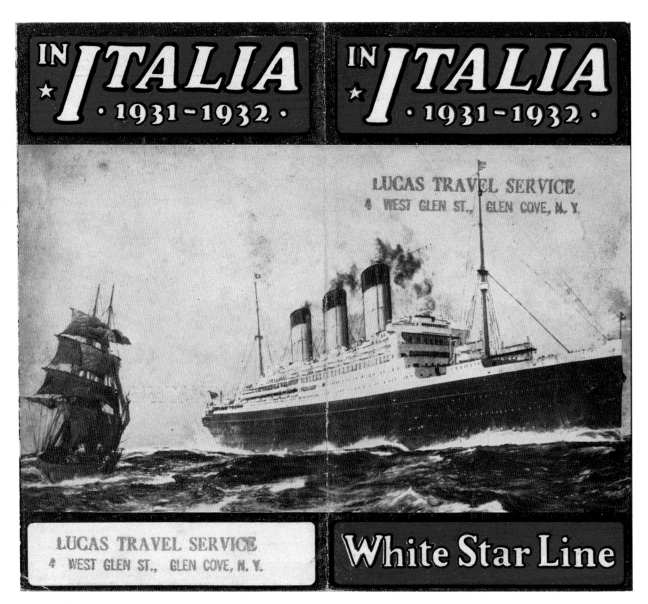

IN *ITALIA*
· 1931-1932 ·

IN *ITALIA*
· 1931-1932 ·

LUCAS TRAVEL SERVICE
4 WEST GLEN ST., GLEN COVE, N. Y.

LUCAS TRAVEL SERVICE
4 WEST GLEN ST., GLEN COVE, N. Y.

White Star Line

An Italian-language brochure of the Majestic, featuring a fine painting by Charles Dixon. When IMM lost the Majestic and got the Leviathan, the funnels of this oil were done over in red, white and blue and the name 'Leviathan' overpainted on the bow.

A fine Fred Hoertz bow-on-view, with a grossly undersized tug.

WHITE STAR LINE
S. S. MAJESTIC
56,551 Tons
The World's Largest Ship

R.M.S. Majestic   *White Star Line*

One of the better Majestic paintings, possibly done by Charles Dixon, British master.

Nearing the end of her career, the Majestic is shown here as operated by Cunard-White Star. Note Aquitania in the left background.

'Cunard White Star'   'Majestic'

tative Fred L. Britten for having menus using French words. The story went around the world, with Britten gaining wide publicity for himself.

Late in the year she ran on the rocks off Staten Island and Captain Herbert Hartley, who had been her master from the beginning, was nicknamed 'Mud Turtle Hartley'. She continually set new speed records, making a number of crossings averaging 25 knots. Because of the government involvement, she was frequently offered for sale, something that did not help advance ticket sales. She raced and beat the *Olympic*. In mid 1925 she sailed with 2,569 passengers on one crossing, more than any ship had carried in either direction since the war. Like both her other Ballin Big Three companion ships, she was selected by countless famous passengers. She reached her peak in 1927, carrying more passengers than either the *Majestic* or the *Berengaria*. The Atlantic conference started listing the average speed of liners in this year. The *Leviathan* was shown

Third Class Smoking Room.

Third Class Dining Room.

The six step-like rises just below funnel No. 2 and No. 1 seen here are the split uptakes joining under each funnel. Photo taken from a shipyard crane just before the stacks were finally given their red, white and blue colours for the first time.

Looking aft from wing of the bridge early in 1923 at Newport News. The nameboard on the starboard side is not yet in place.

as having an average of 23.33 knots; the *Majestic* was shown as averaging 23.06 knots. Commodore Hartley retired in 1927 and was replaced by Captain Harold A. Cunningham.

Two anecdotes of 1927 involved the earliest transatlantic flights, and each has a *Leviathan* connection. The world remembers Charles Lindbergh for his pioneering solo flight to Paris. A few days after that historic flight, the *Leviathan*'s baseball team was playing the London 'Americans' in London. Let engineer Eddie Jones tell what he remembered happening that day:

We were winning. The stands were filled. Suddenly everyone paused

Testing the lifeboat arrangements on C Deck. (Morris Rosenfeld)

Lowering the port lifeboats, stacked three deep forward, at Pier 86, New York (Morris Rosenfeld)

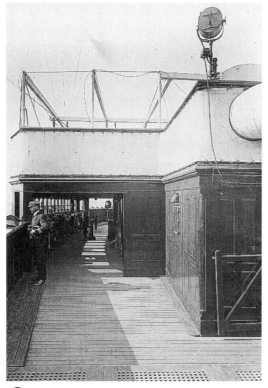

because a deep humming sound could be heard over the London traffic noises. We looked up and there were four dark green bombers in a close formation. British bombers. In the middle, sparkling in the sunlight, was a tiny object. Suddenly we all realized what it was. It was Lindbergh in his 'Spirit of St. Louis'. The bombers had picked him up and were escorting him to Croydon. He had taken off from Paris and was coming to England to sail home on an American cruiser. The stands emptied in seconds and everyone waved and cheered like mad.

Among my favourite artifacts from the *Leviathan* are Eddie Jones' baseball bat and two of his gloves. The bat is painted red, white and blue at its thick end, like the funnels of the *Leviathan*. Eddie Jones was a 'patron' of my six-volume series on the *Leviathan*.

The other choice story involves Clarence

Captain Hartley on the Leviathan's *wide bridge.*

Bridge interior, with battery of engine room telegraphs.

Chamberlin, who with C.A. Levine followed Lindbergh across the Atlantic a few days later. He was given a free passage home on the *Leviathan*, along with Commander Richard E. Byrd, whose plane had been the third to make it across. After sailing home, Chamberlin offered to help the US Lines get publicity for the *Leviathan* by saying he would take off from the ship at sea with mail. He would give the liner another 'first' by announcing the flight as the beginning of air mail delivery from a great liner at sea. US Lines was delighted and had an angular wooden platform built atop the ship's pilot house. It was 60 feet long and about 90 feet above the water. Chamberlin inspected it and asked that it be extended 20 feet. His plan did not include any kind of catapult and was extremely risky at best. Knowing this, US

William Francis Gibbs had to wait until the ship was renovated before she could be dry docked. The Commonwealth dry dock in South Boston was the only dock in America large enough to handle her. Here she makes her grand entrance, spick and span and fresh from her restoration at Newport News, Va. The white lifeboat covers were discarded almost immediately.

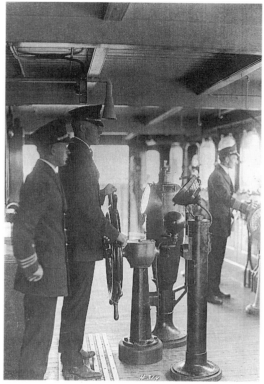

Helmsman and two officers on the bridge.

Most of the hull, like all liners, was really flat, with a curve only at the outer edges. Note the paint barges tied up along the lower left. They were used to carry ten or so painters with paint pots, all working like mad so the red underbody could be painted quickly as the water was pumped out of the dry dock. The Leviathan's draught, after her restoration, was 41 feet, more than any other liner either before or since.

Lines made the requested 20-foot extension by running huge timbers down six and a half decks to the well deck area just aft of the forward deck house.

The idea was for the aeroplane to be hoisted aboard and for the ship to sail out and along the south shore of Long Island on its regular course. Three Navy four-funnel destroyers were recruited to steam along just in case. A bag of mail was prepared for the 'hop off', as it was called. Chamberlin was photographed with his wife, saying goodbye, and all was ready. When the ship was in position, newsreel photographers were alerted on the destroyers, on the bridge and in the crow's nest on the foremast. While cameras turned and everyone held their collective breath, Chamberlin revved his engine and hopped over the wheel chocks, moving down the wet runway. It seemed terribly short, but, when he reached its end, his lift-off was perfect. Rising up like a bird he did roll-overs and loops as everyone cheered. A moving picture of the event clearly showed white plumes of steam coming up from numbers one and two funnels—it was a silent film, and so the whistle salute was not recorded. After some more cavorting, Chamberlin disappeared toward the west. He made it and, today, covers from this flight are highly treasured by stamp people. The stunt was so risky, though, that it was never repeated.

In 1929 the *Leviathan* and all the other ships of US Lines were sold to a financier from Chicago named Paul Wadsworth Chapman. At this point I bought several shares of stock in the new United States Lines Company that Chapman organized. The Chapman era will be remembered for initiating the design of the

Sailing day — the great liner backing out of Pier 86, West 46th Street, New York.

Sister ships — a photo taken from the Majestic showing the Leviathan heading for the open sea. The White Star liner followed an hour later.

Another sailing day — this time the photographer is aboard the Olympic as Leviathan sails, outward bound.

30,000 ton liners *Manhattan* and *Washington*, twin beauties which were to have great impact on the transatlantic scene.

The 'Oiseau Canari' story is a favourite of my *Leviathan* anecdotes. It means Yellow Bird, and was the name of an aeroplane owned by Armand Lotti, wealthy son of a French hotel owner who was determined to fly the Atlantic, despite a French ruling prohibiting such attempts by Frenchmen. The plan to escape from French jurisdiction was worked out like a spy operation. The Yellow Bird took off from Orly airport for what was described as a 'maintenance flight'. Instead, using fuel secretly placed aboard, she crossed the Channel and landed at Southampton. There a well-trained crew dismantled her, loaded her in several trucks and took her in secret to the *Leviathan*'s pier. One of her three-man crew accompanied her to New York, while Lotti and another crew member followed on another

A fine bow view of a Leviathan *sailing*. (Lauren Graham)

Another superb photo, taken from the foredeck of an inbound liner, name unknown. The Leviathan *is shown outward bound.*

An aerial view of Leviathan *coming into Pier 86.* (William J. Green)

Chief Engineer R.L. Harrison, who served only briefly on the Leviathan, *and three of his top assistants, photographed during the ship's trial trip off Cuba in 1923.* (Morris Rosenfeld)

ship. They met, assembled the plane and flew her to an airport in Maine. Everything was done in a highly scientific manner. When they finally took off and found they could not get altitude, the crew was stupefied. What could they do? They were determined to make it, but did not understand why they could not get more than 10 feet or so over the waves. As they were deciding whether to throw overboard their wireless or their food, the truth suddenly dawned. A fourth person was aboard, a stowaway. He was a 22-year-old lad from Portland, Maine. They wanted to throw him overboard, but didn't. And they made it, all the way to their destination—Spain. They were hailed as heroes, having made the fourth non-stop flight from America to Europe. For the stowaway, Arthur Schreiber, it was the greatest moment of his life. George Vecsey, *New York Times* reporter, has documented the story in a fine book on early aviation.

Another chapter in aviation history was written by Dr Lytle S. Adams, who developed what was known at the time as the 'Adams Airmail Pick Up' system. He used the *Leviathan* for his ship-to-shore effort. Thousands of news stories and photos resulted, although real success was infrequent. Eager for publicity, Chapman was happy to welcome what was then described as 'the first direct telephone service from ship to shore'. Three short-wave channels were assigned by the US Radio Commission to the American Telephone and Telegraph Company, and six Bell Telephone Laboratories men went aboard the *Leviathan* on June 29, 1929, to begin tests. Professor H.J. Scott was one of them. He summed it all up like this: 'We commuted on the *Leviathan* every trip during the installation and testing period until the end of December. During this time we were quartered in First Class, which was fine except that it was a nuisance to climb into

Captain Herbert Hartley signed this photo to Mrs Wallace H. White at sea on June 27, 1927. The ship's deck bell seen here in the background is outside the Mariners' Museum, Newport News, Va, at this writing. (Carl A. House)

Women had yet to break into the switchboard operator job category when this photo was taken. The Leviathan's switchboard, May 7, 1923.

Looking forward from funnel Stack No. three — note the astern whistle in the white stripe at the back of No. two funnel. The three-deep nested lifeboats were a continuous maintenance problem.

a tuxedo every night for dinner.' The scene was set for the documentation of the one serious accident the *Leviathan* suffered in her career. More on this shortly.

Where is Miss Leviathan Perfect? That question has vexed me for years, ever since I learned of her birth aboard the *Leviathan* in September, 1929, while the ship's radio telephone experiments were going on aboard. She helped make the all-time record passenger list for the ship, or any liner in the post First World War period. The list, counting Miss Perfect, totalled 2,717 persons. Needless to say her parents named her after the liner.

The Chapman organization was overjoyed at the passenger records being set by the *Leviathan*. Between mid June and mid October, 1929, she carried more people across the Atlantic than any other ship. It was obvious that if she made more trips each year she could

A photo taken by the famed Elmo Pickerill, noted head radio operator on the Leviathan, in mid Atlantic in 1923. Note the hand carved nameboard on the monkey deck rail. Its matching nameboard from the port side was in the Smithsonian Institution in Washington for many years. (Steamship Historical Society of America)

Bellboys stand for inspection, aft on the Boat Deck. Joseph C. Patz, is next to last, at right. He contributed this photo.

Third Class passengers relaxing on a 1924 crossing. They had this after deck area, small indeed, but better than what steerage had. (Otis Oldfield Collection, San Francisco Maritime Museum)

earn more money. Under government ownership she had never exceeded 15 round trips. Plans were now made to operate her for 17½ crossings, but was it physically possible? Heading into winter, the *Leviathan* was being pushed as she had never been pushed before. Her 17th round trip began on December 7, and a large group of reporters were aboard to witness the first regular telephone service between ship at sea and land. Many stories were filed, but none with the impact of those which the correspondents tried to call in on December 12. The storm had built up all the afternoon of the 11th. A north-west gale was blowing, but Commodore Cunningham would not reduce speed. He was going all out, Second Officer Sherman Reed remembered. Reed had called him in his cabin and asked permission to slow down. The response was: 'Maintain your speed, this ship will get in on time, we are not on Hartley's schedule.' Five minutes later Reed saw a wave 40 feet high coming at them.

Passengers in Second Class put on a boxing demonstration, which those in First look down at and enjoy. (Engineer Kenneth Swimm)

Crew swab the Leviathan's Boat Deck. The four-stacker in the upper left, circled by the light fixture, is the famous Mauretania, which the caption at the back of the original photo called 'rival of the Leviathan.' This was during the early days of the Leviathan's operation, when it was claimed that she was not only the world's largest, but also the world's fastest liner.

Just half of the B Deck Promenade is shown here.
All these windows were painted black during the
First World War to make sure enemy submarines
would see no light from this deck. (Morris Rosenfeld)

Sir Thomas Lipton, of America's Cup fame, and Dr
van Angel, the Leviathan's amusement and
entertainment man, in 1925. (Capt. Sherman Reed)

Queen Marie of Romania with Captain Hartley, 1926. (Dr Kerby Martin)

Winifred Hudnut, right, with a fellow passenger on the Leviathan's *Boat Deck.*

Gertrude Hoffman, photographed in 1926 by Dr Kerby Martin, the Leviathan's chief surgeon.

We rode up then went tearing down into the trough, burying our bow deep in the next one. She stopped and shuddered, then a loud crack, like a gun going off. She had split in the middle dropping her forecastle deck four inches, lost her forward island lifeboats and buckled bulkheads. Bridge telephone ringing like mad. No stateroom door in the forward end could be opened.

So Captain Reed would describe the disaster years later. The crack itself happened just forward of the split uptakes, right across C Deck and 16 feet down to D Deck on the starboard side. It was much like the *Majestic*'s crack, which also happened on a December voyage.

Lowering the flag of the US Shipping Board and hoisting the new flag of Paul Wadsworth Chapman's United States Lines Company in 1929.

The 'Club Leviathan' — what the Palm Court looked like after Chapman's designers rebuilt it to be more contemporary. 'Club Leviathan' menus and concert programmes are Art Deco collectors' pieces.

For those interested in the structural weakness that was responsible for these cracks, I urge a perusal of my Volumes III and IV. Reporters seeking to telephone the story to their papers were at first not permitted to use the new device. When threatened by one top editor, Commodore Cunningham gave way and the accounts of the crack were telephoned home. Strange to say, this time, the news stories were not front page. People just could not believe how serious it had been. The split uptakes were partially to blame.

The episode struck the death knell of the Chapman company, coming as it did after the Depression had begun in October, 1929. The IMM ended up buying the *Leviathan* and other US Lines ships, and at long last the sister ships *Leviathan* and *Majestic* ran side-by-side, using the same New York pier. But this did not continue for long, as the White Star Line was once again taken away from IMM and merged with Cunard, meaning a different pairing of two of the Ballin Big Three.

Entering the Rosyth Naval Yard to be scrapped. She made the last crossing under her own power, averaging 17 knots. This one voyage is worth a book all by itself.

The last years of the *Leviathan* were sad ones. The IMM took over where Chapman had left off with the *Manhattan* and the *Washington*, and were no longer interested in the 'world's greatest ship'. To save tonnage port taxes they had her remeasured and used her much lower American tonnage, instead of the inflated British tonnage, a sad blow to those who had always considered her the world's largest ship. American tonnage was based on an old law written before ships had given up sails, and measuring only the hull and one level of deck houses above the hull. By American measurement a liner would be shown as from one-quarter to one-fifth smaller in gross tonnage than by the British rule. This dropped her gross from 59,000 to 48,000. IMM tried to lay her up in 1933, but there was such a public outcry that they were forced to run her for five voyages in 1934. Then she was moved to Hoboken and rusted there until January, 1938, when she steamed, under her own power, to Scotland to be scrapped. Her sale for scrap was a national disgrace in light of the closeness of the Second World War. She would have been worth her weight in gold as a transport in the war, but IMM, which had adopted the name United States Lines, was only interested in the small amount of cash they got for her as scrap. She was being scrapped while the bombs began to fall on Britain. And, strange to say, within sight of the vast hull as it was slowly cut to pieces, was her sister—the *Majestic*, renamed and serving as the world's largest training ship for the British Navy. The ending of these two superb liners makes one of the most mournful stories in maritime annals. Their lives had been all too short.

3

MAJESTIC

The third and largest of Albert Ballin's trio of liners was begun as the *Bismarck*. Completed after the First World War, she is best known as White Star Line's magnificent *Majestic*, long rival with the *Leviathan* for the title of 'World's largest ship'.

A piece of bad luck marred the launching of the *Bismarck* on June 20, 1914. The christening was being done by the Countess Hanna von Bismarck, the late Chancellor Bismarck's granddaughter. At the climax of the ceremony she simply could not break the bottle of champagne, so the Kaiser stepped forward and broke the bottle. Some viewed this as an ill omen. And then came the war. Throughout the conflict the two-thirds finished hull sat at the fitting-out berth, neglected.

The surrender of Germany was followed by the death of Albert Ballin, and the imposition of the harsh peace treaty. There was chaos in Germany at that point. On October 9, 1920, newspaper readers in America were told that the interior of the giant liner had been destroyed by a fire believed to have been of an incendiary origin. On October 30, word came

This view was made for the N.Y. Herald Tribune *in January, 1936. The ship's flag was at half mast because of the passing of King George V. The liner whose forward half is protruding to the right of the* Majestic *looks like* Oriente, *of Ward Line. Note also the White Star house-flag flying above the Cunard house-flag. There's lots in this picture.*

from Hamburg that nothing was being done with the *Bismarck*. Some were urging that she be broken up, so that her steel might be used for other purposes. Three months passed and it was announced in London that the White Star Line had purchased the liner from the British Government, to which she had been given by the Allied Reparations Commission. On March 1, 1921, the maritime press of the world made it known that the *Bismarck* would be renamed *Majestic*. Ballin's last 50,000 tonner was about to begin her career.

At this time the United States was attempting to enforce its new 'Quota System', which stipulated immigration quotas for the different nationalities of the world. Under it, the quota permitted to come to America was to be three per cent of the total of each nationality admitted in 1910. This would cause great difficulties for the shipping lines, because they could not tell when a quota had been filled, and if an immigrant was rejected, shipping lines had to pay the cost of returning him or her.

In the summer of 1921 White Star announced that Commodore Sir Bertram Hayes would command the *Majestic*, and her Chief Engineer would be Joseph Wolfe. Sir Bertram

Kaiser Wilhelm II greeting leading executives of the
Blohm & Voss shipyard at the 1915 christening of
Bismarck. Albert Ballin is the smiling figure in a silk
top-hat, farthest away from the Kaiser among those
just behind him. Ernst Voss is also smiling, bending to
his left, shown just to the left of the Kaiser. The
date is June 20, 1914. (Blohm & Voss)

The tremendous hull of the world's largest liner
poised for the christening. The gaily festooned stand
for dignitaries is already packed. One top-hatted
gentleman poses with two stylishly garbed women at
its back entrance. See the photographer just to the
left of the stand with his tripod. There is no name
on the bow as yet. (Blohm & Voss)

Her sculptured underbody clefts the water for the first time, as shipyard workers crowd the rail aft on D Deck. One is waving. German and Hapag flags flutter atop the building ways. All of Ballin's Big Three are waterborne — his dream is inching toward fulfilment, but war is only three months away — a tragedy (Blohm & Voss)

Now she is three quarters waterborne — eight years will pass before she will be completed. (Blohm & Voss)

had been master of the *Olympic* during the war, and was credited with having sunk two German submarines in one day, one by ramming and the other by gunfire. For this he had received the Distinguished Service Order. Wolfe had been with the company for 23 years, and also had a distinguished record. He headed a team of White Star specialists and Harland & Wolff shipyard executives who were assigned at this time to go to Hamburg to assist in the completion of the *Bismarck/Majestic*. One report published in October, 1921, noted that 'despite the disturbed conditions in Germany there has been no interference with the progress of the work... representatives of the White Star Line and of the German builders are working together to complete the ship, which, in accordance with the terms of the peace treaty, will leave Hamburg as a finished product except for the outfitting with stores and minor equipment.' The extent of the completion was shown by a page of six German photos published by *Marine Engineering* magazine. One view even showed great potted palms in place, another showed table

Afloat, and riding high, the Bismarck *looks much like the* Vaterland *in this view, even to the number and positioning of portholes on the forward deck house.* (Blohm & Voss)

cloths, china and glassware on the Dining Saloon tables, and huge oil paintings were hanging in the Social Hall, not to mention curtains and bedspreads in the royal suite. Blohm & Voss was fulfilling each detail of the treaty.

There were slight differences between the *Bismarck* and the *Vaterland*. As was natural, Albert Ballin had planned to have the third of his Big Three the largest. She would be 956 feet in length overall, instead of 950, although both ships would have a waterline length of 907 feet, and she would be of 56,000 gross tons, 2,000 more than the *Vaterland*. She would have 48 boilers instead of 46 and be capable of generating somewhat more horsepower. Everyone thought she would be the faster of the two. She would most clearly have been the world's largest ship.

Montague S. Black was commissioned by White Star to do a painting of the liner under White Star colours. The resulting work bravely showed masses of smoke pouring out of all three stacks (no one, apparently, told him that the third funnel was a dummy). This painting was used for years as one of the many postcard illustrations of the ship, given out to the public. The originally-estimated 62,000 to 64,000 horsepower was expected to drive the new liner at 23 knots, with some to spare—some thought she might attain nearly 26 knots under favourable weather conditions. All talk

A miscaptioned photo that was run on November 30, 1918, in the New York Tribune. The ship is the Bismarck, but the caption writer called her Moltke. He correctly noted that 'if finished and put in commission [she] would be larger than either the Leviathan or the Imperator.'

Again the same fitting out berth, but now the crane is busy with one of the boilers being lowered into the Bismarck. The huge vessel will be completed and turned over to Britain under the peace treaty. It would be interesting to learn from some reader what the little passenger ship is alongside. (Arnold Kludas)

In the Blohm & Voss floating dry dock, she looks much better now, and a major difference has emerged between Bismarck and Vaterland. The former's dummy funnel has four outside ridges, as the first two have, designed to strengthen the tall funnels. The Vaterland had only one, generally not noticed as it ran up the back of the dummy stack. Note that at this stage the bridge and pilot house are stained mahogany. (Blohm & Voss)

Out of drydock and back at the fitting out berth, and with only the bridge stained mahogany, the ship looks almost ready. See the White Star Line's golden line below the E Deck portholes. Also her D Deck has been painted white and her Smoking Room forward facing is mahogany stained. All but two of the D Deck recessed lifeboats are in position. (Arnold Kludas)

of her being big but of moderate speed was forgotten. Her power plant also kept up with the times—she was being completed as an oil burner, and this was expected to make it possible to develop 91,000 horsepower at 192 revolutions per minute, and there were many diesel auxiliaries. This was not the case for either the *Imperator* or the *Vaterland*. For this reason it is fair to state that the *Vaterland*'s engine plant was the largest steam-turbine plant in the world—ever.

Sir Bertram was ordered to Germany towards the end of March, 1922, to take command of the *Majestic*. He joined the party of White Star people and representatives of Harland & Wolff, who had been in Hamburg almost a year learning about the ship and her engines. Thanks to Mr H. Harland, of the Belfast shipyard bearing his name, and to Chief Engineer Wolfe, relations with the decidedly dispirited Blohm & Voss people had been raised from cool to cordial. Sir Bertram later characterized Wolfe as 'a man whom nothing would put out and who could get on with anybody.' Comments in the German press at this time indicated that the *Bismarck*'s builders and her former owners showed every desire to make her exactly as good as if she were to be used in the German trade. At the same time,

the British let it be known among the workers that the turning over of the ship was simply due to the fact that Germany did not have the money to complete her and put her into commercial service. It was hoped that this would make the work seem easier and go better.

There were many rumours circulating in Hamburg. One was that it had been at first understood that the Reparations Committee was going to hand the *Bismarck* over to the French, a possibility that had angered the Germans. It was darkly hinted that in such an eventuality, the ship would never have left the Elbe. The White Star Commodore also learned that in the final days of the war, all the *Bismarck*'s brass fittings and copper piping had been removed for war purposes. Upon arriving in Hamburg he was told that he and his party were guests of the German Government until the ship's trials were finished. 'We were guests no doubt, but it did not appear that our hosts had made very strenuous efforts to shine as such', he wrote in his autobiography, *Hull Down*. His cabin, and those of Mr A.B. Cauty,

Being towed stern first away from the yard to commence her trip down the Elbe to Cuxhaven. The tug Wendemuth *will go all the way with her.* (Arnold Kludas)

Four tugs assist. (Arnold Kludas)

the White Star Line general manager, Mr
Wilding, of Harland & Wolff, and Mr Harland, were not ready for use, but were filled
with odds and ends. The Commodore's stateroom did not even have a bed, and it was full
of spare wash basins. Chief Steward J.O. Jennings, part of the take-over group, was a man
of infinite resources and soon made everyone
comfortable, Sir Bertram remembered.

When the *Bismarck* was ready to leave the
yard, the banks of the Elbe were crowded with
thousands watching and weeping. Several
small craft with young men singing sad
laments were paddling around the huge ship
as she moved down river, the Commodore
noted. Someone managed to dab a red skull
and cross bones along the ship's lower hull,
as an illustration of how he felt, and quite
understandably. The liner ran aground, but was
freed by a high tide. Two Belgian tugs assisted
her to manoeuvre around the bends. Many of
the British crew aboard, and even more in
England, were fearful that the vessel would
be sabotaged like the German Battle Fleet had
been at Scapa Flow.

The trials were to be off the Bight of Heli-
goland, and they took place on March 28. No
flags were flying. Captain Hans Ruser, who
had commanded both of the earlier Big Three,
was on the Bridge. He had become a partner
in a prosperous wine business. All that was
required of the ship was that she prove she
could produce her 66,000 horsepower. She
steamed for three hours, made this goal with
ease, and headed back to anchorage off Cuxhaven. Sir Bertram and the other British representatives asked that certain experiments be
made to test her turning and stopping qualities, and these were done to their complete
satisfaction. 'I must say', he wrote, 'she exceeded our expectations in every way and
proved herself to be a very handy ship.'

An extra week was allowed for the Germans
to complete her passenger accommodations.
A thank you lunch was then given to the Blohm
& Voss officials at a Hamburg hotel, which
concluded with speeches and a good feeling
all around. The remainder of the ship's British crew arrived from Southampton, but were
not allowed aboard until the Germans had all
left. The leave-taking was 'really pathetic', Sir
Bertram confided to his journal. Afterward the
name *Bismarck* was painted over on the bows

Now the Smoking Room face is white, but the pilot house remains mahogany. The beautiful ship is resting quietly at anchor off Cuxhaven ready for her trials. The tug Wendemuth is still with her as she takes on oil from a small tanker on her port side. The stacks still gleam in their Hapag yellow-buff. (Blohm & Voss)

Another view at anchor. A tug is taking up a position on her bow, but the same small tanker is alongside. A gangway stands ready for use to board or debark crew at her open side port aft on the port side. (Blohm & Voss)

Still at anchor with the after side port still open.
(Hapag-Lloyd)

A starboard broadside, with a four-masted bark in the distance off her stern, the Bismarck is still anchored. (Arnold Kludas)

Eight views featured in a US monthly in October, 1921; taken while the Bismarck was still in German hands. They show how well she was finished by the Hamburg craftsmen. The great paintings shown in the top left view may have been put in place just to make the Social Hall look more elegant.

S. S. Majestic: Interior Views of First-Class Accommodations. (1) Lounge. (2) Dining Saloon. (3) Ritz-Carlton Restaurant. (4) Palm Court and Entrance to Ritz-Carlton Restaurant. (5) Reading and Writing Room. (6) Stateroom en Suite. (7) Smoking Room. (8) Swimming Pool.

Another pre-British view aboard Bismarck. The Social Hall minus the oil paintings showing lamp clusters in their place. A view looking toward the stage and grand piano (forward). (Blohm & Voss)

and stern, and *Majestic* substituted. With White Star colours on the three tremendous funnels, the ship put out to sea. It was a fine Sunday morning, April 9, 1922. 'With my flag as Commodore at the mainmast-head, we sailed for Southampton. We arrived safely the next day', Sir Bertram added. P.A.S. Franklin, President of the International Mercantile Marine, owners of White Star Line, was there to welcome the liner. He wired home: 'Delighted with the *Majestic*. She is most satisfactory and far exceeds expectations. Public rooms, deck spaces and accommodations generally exceedingly good. Speed trials very satisfactory. Satisfied she will comfortably exceed 25 knots at sea, but of course she will not be run at top speed on early voyages.'

In due course it emerged that she had made 80,000 horsepower at 180 rpms on her way to Southampton. While she was not pushed, she made nearer 25 knots than 23. Engineers familiar with the ship claimed that she could develop a maximum of 100,000 horsepower,

and that 'with such power she could make a stab at the *Mauretania*'s record with reasonable assurance of success.' Sir Arthur H. Rostron, the famous Cunarder's captain, was quoted as saying that his ship's speed potential had been upped by her conversion to burn oil. He added: 'When my owners give the word she will be let out.' And that is just what did happen two years later.

The maiden voyage of the *Majestic* had been set for May 10, and she had less than a month to be outfitted. Everything was done on a gigantic scale. Three thousand mattresses were brought aboard, as were 17 tons of blankets, 2,700 pillows and 1,500 bolsters, 75 tons of dishes, cooking utensils and bedroom crockery, more than three tons of silverware and cutlery... 190,000 pieces of linen, from napkins and doilys to expensive bedspreads, and 77,000 towels, 13,000 pillow cases, 8,000 bedspreads, 11,000 sheets... and so on. If the linen required were to have been spread out on the ground, it would have covered 50 acres. If hung on a single line, side by side, the pieces would have extended 162 miles. By May 9 a number of her most famous passengers had arrived and were aboard. There was Lord Inchcape, chairman of the Peninsular and

Looking aft toward the great double glass doors leading into the main stairway on B Deck. Notice the tremendous rug in the centre, overlaying an even larger carpet; and the rich panelling. A Blohm & Voss caption modestly calls the great room the 'Hall'. (Blohm & Voss)

Palms in the Winter Garden, along with cane furniture: looking aft toward the raised à la carte restaurant. It was never called the Ritz Carlton, as it had been on both Imperator and Vaterland/Leviathan. It went without a name for some time, eventually coming to be known as the Parisian Restaurant. (Blohm & Voss)

The Bismarck's Second Class Dining Saloon, photographed before the ship was turned over to White Star. (Blohm & Voss)

Oriental Company, Harold A. Sanderson, chairman of the White Star line, and H. Harland of Harland & Wolff. Also Herbert Pulitzer, Cyres H. McCormick and H.B. Thayer. They made a brave show of it, but the passenger list was not a large one—perhaps it was too similar to the maiden voyage of another White Star giantess—the *Titanic*. Only 655 were to sail the next day, 362 in First, 127 in Second and 166 in Third. Her capacity was over 4,000.

One unexpected incident marred the maiden voyage, but few heard about it. One of the ship's port turbines had to have new supports made and installed during the crossing. This was done by her engine room crew without comment, a fine repair job at sea. Upon her arrival on May 17 at New York one news report led off by noting that she could claim 'the glory of knowing that she had made the swiftest maiden trip of any liner from Cherbourg.' She had covered the 3,058 miles at an average of 22.69 knots, in 5 days, 14 hours and 45 minutes. 'This is not great, but it is fine for an untried ship', wrote another reporter. He added: 'Captain Hayes said that she never had been pushed and that on the few fair days of the run she had made slightly more than 25

The Majestic, *swinging at anchor off Quarantine, while the sleek* Mauretania *passes, outward bound. This is the ending of the White Star liner's maiden voyage with all its talk about her challenging the Cunarder's Atlantic speed supremacy. The photo is taken from the N.Y. Tribune's rotogravure section.*

Maiden arrival photo with seaplane. The Pacific & Atlantic photo caption notes that 'the giantess seemingly covers a distance equal to that between the Singer and Municipal buildings'.

A rotogravure section view of the docking. Moments later the Majestic would bash in a portion of the top deck of the pier. Note the White Star house-flag in a white circle at the ends of the name scroll design on the counter stern, a decoration that replaced the original seal of Hamburg.

It would be hard to find a more majestic view of a great liner docking than this Herbert Photo. It shows a December 1926 arrival of Majestic, a day late because of storms on the Atlantic, and further delayed by fog below the Battery. She brought a large cargo of Christmas mail. Taken by Herbert Photos, this view is a classic.

knots and he felt pretty sure that after limbering up she would come pretty close to being the swiftest liner afloat.' Every ship in the harbour greeted the *Majestic* 'vaporously', as one paper put it.

The *Reliance*, of United American Line, passed the *Majestic* near Ambrose, letting go with her siren. Sir Bertram acknowledged with three long blasts. The *Reliance*, a beautiful three-funnelled, 20,000-ton liner, had been designed by the Hamburg American Line and was something of a little sister to *Vaterland/Bismarck*, with split uptakes and a similar outline. She had come under American ownership after the war. The first ship to meet the *Majestic* within the harbour was the heroic speed queen *Mauretania*, outward bound. The two ships, rivals for the Blue Riband, saluted by dipping their ensigns, nothing more. A

Four of the world's largest three-stackers in one view. The Leviathan *and* Statendam *can be seen over in Hoboken. The* Majestic *and* Belgenland *are at the IMM Chelsea piers, along with the* Britannic *and either the* Manhattan *or the* Washington.

minor embarrassment, brushed aside as trivial in most stories, happened while the new ship was entering the slip at White Star's Hudson River pier. She stove in a 12-foot section of the corrugated pier shed and drove a crowd of well wishers in confusion from the bulkhead. One story said the damage amounted to a few hundred dollars. The ship had been just inching in. She was secure at 4.22 pm, having been warped into the slip in only 24 minutes. There was a spirit of forgiveness for the 'talented Teutons' who had put the hull of the splendid liner together, one reporter opined. Nothing occurred on the maiden venture, he added, and 'no bombs were discovered in the remote corners of the giant liner'. The comment of the experts was that the *Majestic* 'was a perfect specimen of craftsmanship, considered merely from the exterior, and that never in the annals of seagoing craft had any of the type come into the harbour with "sweeter lines".' The rotogravure sections of the major New York papers the next Sunday were filled with pictures of the *Majestic*.

A feature article in *Marine Engineering* for

Six great liners together — two of which would have the same name in due course. Bottom to top: Berengaria docking, Majestic, Caledonia, Lancastria, Ile de France and Conte di Savoia. Who would have thought that the Majestic would eventually be renamed Caledonia? This photo was taken shortly after the merger of White Star and Cunard.

June, 1922, showed a large photo of the Social Hall. The huge oil paintings that had been hanging in the 1921 set of *Bismarck* interiors were missing—perhaps White Star thought they were too German, or maybe they had been put there by Hapag just for the German photographers, and then taken back to some museum. It is interesting how the *Majestic*'s split uptakes were hailed now that the ship was flying the British flag. The IMM house organ, *The Ocean Ferry*, stated: 'This 250-feet of clear space through the centre of the ship is an arrangement, unlike any other ship now in commission, and is made possible by a novel construction of the smoke stacks, which are divided and brought up on the sides of the ship

A very artificial, yet interesting, view of Majestic put out by Cunard White Star's publicity department. Obviously a cut out photo of the ship superimposed over another of the skyline. Note the touch up man's error when he put smoke coming out of the third, dummy, funnel.

until they reach the upper deck.' The *Leviathan* was not in commission at this time.

One of the best known of the senior White Star staff aboard was Dr J.H. Beaumont, Chief Surgeon. He had been aboard the *Olympic* when she had gone to the aid of the British battleship *Audacious*, which had struck a mine off Ireland and had been sinking. The *Olympic* had taken her in tow, but had had to cut her loose when she began to founder. She sank. *Olympic* had been ordered into a remote port in the north Ireland, and every person aboard had been put under oath not to divulge the extent of the 'misadventure' to the *Audacious*.

In July the *Majestic* set a new westbound record from Cherbourg of 5 days, 8 hours and 9 minutes. She would better this in late November, with a 5 day, 6 hour and 13 minute passage, but she never came close to the *Mauretania*'s pre-war Atlantic speed record. In fact, as time passed she would prove to be slightly slower than the *Leviathan*.

One of the exciting events of *Majestic*'s career took place when she was anchored near the Royal Yacht *Victoria and Albert*, during the Cowes Week regatta. King George V and Queen Mary with their son Prince George were brought over from the yacht, and the royal Standard was raised on *Majestic*'s mainmast.

The Majestic in Southampton waters. Docked behind the Olympic, a photo taken May 22, 1922.

This photo was published by the Southampton Industrial Archaeology Group. It shows Majestic outward bound, passing Calshot with tugs. The seaplane in the foreground was a competitor for the Schneider Trophy in 1929.

A photo signed by many of her top officers, shows Majestic when Captain William Marshall was her master. Chief Engineer Wolfe's signature is barely visible at the top right.

The Majestic and Leviathan together at Southampton, with a bow view of Mauretania to the right.

A training flight flying over the Majestic as she approached her pier at Southampton on February 12, 1936, on her next to last eastbound crossing. The Imperial Airways flying boat will be participating in 1937 in a new transatlantic service by air, the Acme Newspicture photo caption said. Two Union Castle liners are docked above the White Star liner, and a Lamport & Holt cruising liner is at the top to the left.

The King was in naval uniform, with a solid gold band and four thin gold bands on each sleeve. Hosting were Harold Sanderson and Sir Bertram. A special feature was a display of diving and swimming in the ship's great pool by Miss Winnie Elliott, the *Majestic*'s 'official mermaid'. Lord Louis Mountbatten and his bride, the former Miss Edwina Ashley, made their honeymoon on the *Majestic* in September, 1922.

On October 25, 1922, Sir Bertram spoke to an estimated 100,000 American listeners over Radio Station WJZ, Newark, New Jersey. He was joined on the air by Chief Steward Jennings. It was believed that due to the night being cold and clear, their words were carried to points west of the Mississippi and as far south as Cuba. Sir Bertram described the work of his principal assistants among his staff of 1,064 men and 28 women. Mr Jennings went into matters of 'housekeeping' on the world's largest ship. Dr Beaumont also participated, but, due to a cold, he was unable to sing some of his own compositions as he had expected to do.

At the time the world's largest dry dock was in Boston, Mass. The *Majestic* went there in November 1922, for new propellers and to have her hull painted (which took 14 tons of paint). During the dry docking, two of the 12-inch steel cables used to guide her snapped, with

reports like field-pieces. One of the ends lashed back toward the ship like a giant whip, cutting down an electric light pole as if it had been a weed. A humorist of the day, Baron Munchausen, was so impressed with the size of the *Majestic* that he wrote as follows: 'She is so big that they have to run a dredge ahead of her so as to get her through the ocean. When you go "topside" you can see the Woolworth building ahead and the Eiffel Tower astern. They turned her around the first trip and knocked Ireland 50 miles nearer England. On a clear day you can see the tops of the funnels. . . .'

Those in First Class on the *Majestic* who did not wish to eat in the luxurious domed Dining Saloon could take their meals in the elegant restaurant, 'for a very moderate additional cost', D.M.A. Pelligrin, the restaurant manager, said in an interview in May, 1923. In fact, he added, the difference could be as little as two pounds, five shillings (or $10) for the five and a half day crossing. One advantage of eating in the restaurant was that meals

Being pulled, and pushed, into the mammoth dry dock at South Boston, with 14 tugs helping. Note the three four-masted barques and the five three-masted coastal barges at anchor. (Underwood & Underwood)

A dramatic bow on view. (George H. Davis, Jr)

could be ordered at any time from 8 am to 11 pm There were 78 in the restaurant staff, including a 'palm court attendant'.

Another speed record was set by the *Majestic* from New York to Cherbourg, this time with an average speed of 24.79 knots. She and the *Leviathan*, out in mid 1923, were showing that only the *Mauretania* could beat them, establishing themselves clearly as the second and third fastest ships on the Atlantic — which meant in the world.

From the sublime to the ridiculous: five men were required to roll back the 25-foot long, 1,000 pound rose velvet carpet in the *Majestic*'s Social Hall. It took ten men to lift it. Every evening except Sunday this space was cleared, baring the parquet floor of oak and walnut for dancing. The 25 by 50 foot dancing space could accommodate from 60 to 100 couples. This was elegance at sea. The *Majestic* car-

ried more passengers in 1923 than any other ship—37,876. She also carried on one passage 843 in First Class, the largest number in that class in the year. She was succeeding. It was also said that she handled more radio messages than any other ship. In a single transatlantic voyage, her operators would send 3,000 messages, aggregating 40,000 words—in one day she handled 350 messages in 10 hours. On December 11, 1924, the White Star flagship brought in to New York the largest winter list of the year—669 in First, 528 in Second and 504 in Third, plus 10,000 sacks of Christmas mail. She sailed home with 1,678 passengers and her agent could boast: 'No ship has ever done a better winter business.'

Ellen Jeffrey, who runs the smart New York gift shop, said she once had a customer who bought her entire trousseau from the shipboard store. 'My what a good time we had. Her young man was almost jealous before we were through, she got so interested in clothes.' On another crossing a baby was born, and 'I think

A very fine close-up, as workers tie the many hawsers to drydock bollards. (George H. Davis)

The open end of the drydock is closed by moving a huge caisson into place. Tugs pull and push it, with men riding in on its top. (George H. Davis)

Great timbers are wedged on either side to hold the liner in place, while the water is pumped out.
(George H. Davis)

every passenger on the *Majestic* came in to get something for it.'

Masseur George Bell and his two 'electric baths' were all the rage on the White Star flagship. In use from 6 am to 7 pm they looked like huge electric washing machines, but opened up for a person to sit inside, with only the head showing. The treatment started with 15 minutes at a temperature of 175 degrees; then a hot shower and a brisk Swedish massage, a thorough soaping and another hot shower, a gradual application of cold water, an hour's cooling in a rest room, and you ended with 'a luxurious feeling of well being.' George's wife was masseuse on the *Majestic*, and his son did the same on the *Olympic*.

In the summer of 1924, 500 delegates to the Democratic National Convention, being held in New York, came aboard for dinner. One,

in a speech of thanks, concluded: 'We are proud to be here on this fine sea-borne palace, the greatest ship under the American flag (*sic*).' Sir Bertram Hayes retired in December, 1924, being replaced by Captain George Metcalfe. Among the many parting gifts Sir Bertram received was a gold-topped ebony walking stick, a present from the Sandy Hook pilots.

Late in 1924 the *Majestic* suffered the only serious accident in her life. She cracked amidships, revealing a structural weakness that both she and the *Leviathan* had. The crack took place on December 14, a day out of New York, on C Deck, and went 100 feet from starboard to port, extending down the port side to the rim of a porthole on Deck D. She would not sail again until April 21. In due course an editorial in *Marine Engineering* magazine con-

The hull is scraped and a new waterline painted.
(Keystone View Co)

The 60,000-ton Southern Railway floating dock lifted the White Star liner on April 3, 1925, at Southampton. Nine tugs helped out. (Pacific & Atlantic)

A postcard showing the dock after its 18,000 tons of water had been pumped out to lift the 56,000 gross ton liner. The photo was published in the N.Y. Tribune on April 12, 1925.

demned the great secrecy which had surrounded this affair. 'As a consequence,' the magazine explained, 'the naval architect is usually enabled to learn little or nothing from the defects found in operation of ships other than those belonging to his own company.'

On May 14, 1925, Dr Ernst Foerster, consulting engineer for Hapag, said that the *Majestic* was larger than the *Leviathan*. The two sister ships had both laid claim to being the 'largest ship in the world.' Dr Foerster explained that the change in design needed to make the *Bismarck* six feet longer 'entailed enormous expense.' He also noted that 'the *Majestic* would have a greater tonnage than the *Leviathan* if they both used the same method of measurement.' He did not know the tricks that William Francis Gibbs had discovered about tonnage measurement.

Despite a strike of British seamen, the *Majestic* sailed on September 2, 1925, with 2,402 westbound passengers, the largest list since 1914. Each of the Ballin Big Three was setting records almost continuously on the passenger-carrying front. All three were quite successful from this standpoint.

Arriving on the *Majestic* on August 3, 1926, after a visit to England, P.A.S. Franklin made a startling announcement. There was to be a new mammoth White Star steamer 'of the largest class'. It was expected that she would be called *Oceanic*, and her tonnage would be around 60,000 gross. She would take three and a half years to build, and would have a speed of around 25 knots. Harland & Wolff would build her, and she was expected to have 'a family resemblance to the handsome *Olympic*', he said.

White Star also made news in a very small way around this time by announcing that Second Class on the *Majestic* would have a manicurist, Miss Queenie Cuy, of Bournemouth, and her chair was to be in the Second Class Barber Shop. A man named Willis Jackson had a unique assignment with White Star. He was the 'Master of Salutation' for that company, and the liners that were part of the IMM combine. He worked at their main office, 1 Broadway, New York, and when any of the IMM ships came into sight off Quarantine, he would hurry to the rooftop ready to acknowledge the ship's flag salute with the company house flag. He had seven different houseflags to handle, representing Atlantic Transport Line, Leyland Line, Panama Pacific Line, White Star-Dominion Line, White Star Line, White Star-American Line and Red Star Line.

On board the *Majestic* there was another specialist proud of his work, Charles Alcock, Librarian and Sacristan. Since May, 1922, he had assisted at 1,453 masses aboard, officiated at by 290 priests. There had been 2,856 communions received by passengers, and ten bishops had helped out. Another specialist whose name had gained wide credance because of the *Majestic* was the British marine artist Walter Thomas. His superb three-quarters portrait of the liner had become one of the best known pieces of pictorial shipping art of the day, and hung in countless offices and travel agencies around the world.

Also in 1926, the *Majestic* carried more passengers than any other ship. This honour was bounced back and forth between Ballin's Big Three. The *Majestic*'s 1926 record was 37,800. There were 422 sailings on the Atlantic that year by IMM ships, and the total number carried by the member lines was 188,194.

A major development occurred as 1927 began. The Royal Mail Line, one of Britain's oldest and most historic steamship companies, bought White Star Line. It was all part of a massive stock transaction and would soon end in disaster. It was symptomatic of the downward trend that industry observers knew was happening within White Star. On the surface, however, all seemed serene. An aerial photograph taken on January 18, 1927, showed the 'Magnificent Trio' berthed together at Southampton. The *Majestic* was to sail the following day; the *Homeric* would depart January 22, and the *Olympic* was being given her annual overhaul.

The IMM house organ contained two features each month that were always of interest to *Majestic* fanciers. One was a page of photos of famous personalities who sailed on IMM ships, and there were many who chose the *Majestic*. Ignace Paderewski, pianist and Polish patriot, was shown in his winter coat with large fur collar. Feodor Chaliapin, Russian

RMS Majestic *in mid ocean, a snapshot taken by S. Marphee of the Olympic.*

A view of storm damage on the Majestic in 1929. This photo was released by the Associated Press. It shows bent cargo booms atop the forward deck house.

This Acme photo used in the Herald Tribune *shows a smashed cargo boom support, with the ship's superstructure rising in the background. Published January 17, 1929. (Acme Photo)*

basso, looked very young and healthy, in a massive sort of way. There was Prince Chichibu, brother of the Emperor of Japan, a very small, very proper personality. Also there was Charles Dana Gibson, famous American artist, with Mrs Gibson, a sister of Lady Astor. Another regular feature was the letters to the editor column. A.J. Warner, drama editor of the *Rochester* (NY) *Times-Union* wrote to say how his voyage on the White Star flagship had been 'exceptionally comfortable'. He said that the restaurant was equal 'to the best Paris or London could offer'. The magazine also had many titbits, such as the paragraph about the King and Queen of Afghanistan visiting the *Majestic* and being most impressed with the great pool; and nice little picture stories, like the one about the young women from Cornell University who were given a tour through the *Majestic*'s kitchens. They were studying New York's markets, hotels and railroad terminals, to get to know how to feed people in large numbers.

White Star tried to keep ahead with new ideas. Passengers on the *Majestic* who arrived June 28, 1928, at Cherbourg, were the first to have a direct air service connection with Paris available. The planes used were one-seater Farman-Goliath machines which had large upholstered wicker chairs. The fare: £10 ($40).

Ship news reporters were always eager to view the *Majestic*. There was usually a story, such as the time Dr A.S.W. Rosenback brought the manuscript of *Alice in Wonderland* home with him. He had bought it for $75,000 in London. The *Majestic* was always breaking records, such as on September 11, 1928, when she docked with 2,580, a record for the year. Or there would be news of the new White Star superliner. In December it was announced that she would have diesel propulsion.

Once in a while the *Majestic* would have a new master, as when Capt. Metcalfe had to retire for ill health, and was replaced by Capt. William Marshall. Major H.O.D. Seagrave, the British racing car driver, was always news. On January 9, 1929, he brought his new speedboat, named *Miss England*, over to America on the *Majestic*. He also had his latest car, the 'Golden Arrow', along for another spin at Daytona Beach.

When the news was really scarce, the alert reporter could usually find a feature about some odd assignment connected with the *Majestic*. For example during the two days before her every arrival, there would be over

A crew member was killed on December 23, 1932, when this damage was done to the Third Class pantry on Majestic. *His name was J.H. Johnston and he was crushed against the steel bulkhead of the pantry on the opposite side of the forward deckhouse.* (Acme Photo)

5,000 telephone calls from friends or relatives of the 2,000 incoming passengers about the time of her docking. The White Star night operator was William Williamson, and a very busy man he always was on these occasions. And then the big ship was continually being refurbished. In March, 1929, 50 new bathrooms were added to meet the continuing demand for de luxe accommodations. At the same time, each Third Class cabin was fitted with an electric call bell.

Now and then there was a sad story, such as on September 26, 1929, when White Star made known that it had deferred work on the new *Oceanic*, a ship that would never be finished. The new White Star owner, Lord Kylsant, turned out to be more of a promoter than a shipping man. His débâcle gave maritime writers much material. In fact White Star had to be repossessed by IMM.

In early 1930, Capt. Marshall was named Commodore of White Star Line, a post which had not been filled since the departure of Sir

Bertram Hayes. This entitled the *Majestic* to fly a special flag, a White Star house flag edged with white. On February 14, 1930, the *Majestic* opened the first public service of radio telephone by liner to Great Britain, with special permission of the British Post Office. Captain P.R. Vaughan, assistant commander, rang up the company office in London and talked with General Manager Cauty.

A most clever star map was devised by Capt. S.S. Stubbs, first officer of the *Majestic*. Published by Hammond, it showed for every hour of the year the visible stars. Movable discs, openings on the cover etc. made this amazing facility work.

Despite the Depression, famous personages continued to sail on the *Majestic*. There was a wonderful photo of Marie Dressler, comedienne, holding a life belt—what a mischievous smile on her face. And 'The Ocean Ferry' had a whole page of photos showing how the ship's deck tennis champion, Second Engineer Joseph Brown, defeated world famous tennis ace Helen Wills Moody. The *New York American*'s ship news reporter, Harry Acton, had a good idea one time when he was at a midnight sailing of the *Majestic*. Why not charge visitors, and give the proceeds to seamen's welfare? No sooner said than done.

The Depression cut Atlantic travel down by more than half. Steamship ads became much more 'hard sell'. A *Majestic* notice published on September 30, 1931, showed a picture of a cabin with two lovely bedsteads. The text: '$122.50 buys a passage to Europe in a room like this.'

A seat at the table of Dr Beaumont was one of the most highly prized and joyously accepted tributes any *Majestic* passenger could wish for. The witty Scotsman's conversation meant never a dull moment: 'Blondes are better sailors than brunettes...perhaps that is why gentlemen prefer them.' As to growing old, he advised: 'Never entertain the thought.' Real life was was often stranger than fiction, as an A.G. Christensen story proved. He was head of the Southampton passenger service section in New York. One time in late 1930 Mary and Margaret Gibb, who were Siamese twins, wanted passage on the *Majestic*, but

insisted on having a single ticket and one fare. After Mr Christensen had explained how many meals there were during the trip and how expensive it was to serve two mouths, the twins said they would gladly pay for two tickets. A portable nine-hole miniature golf course was installed on the White Star flagship late that year and proved extremely popular. In good weather it was set out on deck, at other times in the lounge. Chief Engineer Joseph Wolfe resigned at the end of 1930, and was replaced by his second in command, Morris L. Evans, whose nickname was 'Taffy'.

Richard Halliburton, traveller and author, sailed in March, 1931, on the *Majestic*, with his aeroplane, the 'Flying Carpet', on the first leg of a two-year around the world voyage. This was the year the *Leviathan* beat the *Majestic* in a head-to-head race across the Atlantic by 3 hours, 45 minutes. On May 26, 1931, a vast fleet of 672 US Army aircraft flew over the *Majestic* and other liners docked at New York in a special display of air power.

Armchairs replace the old style swivel chairs in a restyled Tourist Dining Saloon on the ship in mid 1931. A portable dance floor 425 square

A night view taken on February 17, 1931, showing the Majestic *in the floating dry dock at Southampton. The caption called it 'an unusual night view'.*

A 1933 dry docking, with Olympic in view above.

feet in size was made for the à la carte restaurant, created from 236,940 separate pieces of oak, walnut, mahogany, maple and rosewood glued and hydraulically compressed to a canvas backing. Talking picture equipment was installed for First and Tourist classes in August of the same year.

The short week-end cruise came into its own in 1931. The *Majestic* made her first on August 20, from New York to Nova Scotia. Prices began at $35 and included meals, stateroom and 'every necessity'. And there was the 'One Day Cruise'. The price of $15 'entitled you to every facility on this famous White Star liner'. The ship sailed out to sea on Wednesday night, October 21, returning Thursday evening—24 full hours afloat. The Vacuum Oil Co. sponsored a dinner aboard the *Majestic* on September 9, 1931, dedicated to international commerce, and included a network radio broadcast from the ship. In October another

Depression-oriented step was taken: the entire Second Class area was converted to Tourist.

One of IMM's most valuable publicity assets was the pen of a young Englishman, William Seabrook. His cartoon-like sketches of officers, passengers and company people were a much enjoyed feature of *The Ocean Ferry*. A typical drawing he did featured Henry Bushnell and Alfred Murray, saloon deckmen. He showed them in their regular place at the *Majestic*'s gangway, where they had graciously officiated since she entered service in 1922. Another cartoonist, Billie De Beck, creator of the famed character Barney Google, dashed off a sketch moments before the gangway was lowered, on his fifth *Majestic* crossing. It showed the name 'Majestic' on the gangplank, and Barney trying to pull his famous horse, Spark Plug, up the gangway. The wording in the 'cloud' overhead read: 'Come on—you're gonna have your oats at the Captain's table an everything.'

The *Majestic* sailed on December 31, 1931 with 1,225 passengers on a New Year's cruise out of New York. A number of professional entertainers were aboard. Frank Sutton, the ship's stenographer, made a few headlines in March, 1932. He often worked for a dozen people on one trip. He had served Lord Trenchard, head of Scotland Yard (and founder of the RAF), and Winston Churchill, on their crossings. He could take up to 200 words a minute.

In 1932 the IMM acquired the *Leviathan*. For a short period, two years, two of Albert Ballin's Big Three sailed under the same management. The disastrous failure of the Royal Mail had thrown the White Star Line back under the IMM fold, and both *Leviathan* and *Majestic* docked at the same Chelsea piers at New York. A comparison of the passenger totals for these two ships in the Depression year of 1932 is interesting. Within this period the *Majestic* made one extra crossing. Their eastbound trips showed quite a range, from a low of 125 passengers who sailed on October 18 on the *Leviathan*, to a high of 1,553 sailing on June 28, also on the United States Lines' flagship. The *Majestic* recorded her lowest list on September 7, when 226 sailed with her, and her high was the June 22 sailing, when she took out 1,106.

A slight change in the appearance of the *Majestic* was made at this time, when her entire hull was painted black in the 1932 overhaul. The white top strake was eliminated. The famous White Star gold line remained, a symbol of elegance. These were days when cost cutting was vital—it is common gossip that White Star ships were painted only on the side facing the piers. A sad comedown for one of the greatest of all the liner companies.

A particularly large and grand brochure was issued by White Star for *Majestic* cruises at this point. It measured 14″ × 12½″ and spread out the 42½″ × 37″. Green tinted, it boasted monster pictures of the ship's public rooms. The ship made three four-day cruises in the winter of 1932-1933, with prices beginning at $50, the destination being either Nassau or Bermuda.

In 1933 Prince Serge Ouroussow was made the 'official host' of the *Majestic*. Formerly a lieutenant in the Russian Imperial Navy, and for 15 years in diplomatic service, he was in charge of arranging deck sports, dances and other social activities for all three classes. The liner gained some notoriety at this time by being charged in newspaper stories with 'bringing illegal liquor' to the United States.

A picture of the *Majestic's* Chief Chef John Pearse appeared in *Marine News* magazine in February, 1934, along with a splendid breakfast menu from the ship. American breakfast foods were offered, including Wheatena, Hecker H-O Oats, Heinz Rice Flakes, Grape Nuts, Quaker Crackels, Force, Post's Bran Flakes, Puffed Wheat, Post Toasties, Breakfast Bran, Rice Krispies, Corn Flakes and Puffed Rice. For those who wanted the real thing, there was Scotch Oatmeal Porridge.

Morris L. Evans, Chief Engineer, exposed a company secret in an interview published on June 24, 1934. He said that passengers who talked glibly about speeding up big ships had no idea of the increase in consumption of fuel involved. As illustration, he said, on the previous westward crossing the *Majestic's* regu-

Captain R.B. Irving, one of the Majestic's *many masters, photographed by Robert E. Coates.*

The *Majestic* with a convoy
of tugs, in New York Harbor

J. P. Wolfe, the *Majestic's*
Chief Engineer

Gargoyle Marine Oils

Lubricate the "Majestic"

Chief Engineer J. P. Wolfe of the White Star Liner *Majestic* is in command of one of the mightiest power plants afloat. This power plant, for 6½ years has driven the *Majestic's* 56,000 tons at a running speed of 25 knots—crossing the Atlantic in 5½ days.

It's a story of powerful machinery giving a huge liner tremendous speed—a story of engine efficiency at its highest. For the *Majestic's* fine performances could never have been accomplished without the perfect functioning of her vast propelling machinery.

Chief Engineer Wolfe uses Gargoyle Marine Oils to lubricate the *Majestic's* mighty engines. He is one of the many experienced marine engineers who have learned

by their own tests the practical qualities of efficiency and economy which distinguish these world-wide lubricants; who have learned, specifically, that Gargoyle Marine Oils decrease friction, increase speed, and reduce the quantity of oil consumed.

Gargoyle Marine Oils can be procured in more than 300 of the world's ports. In each of these ports—the leading harbors of the seven seas—there is a Vacuum Oil representative. He is familiar with every type of marine machinery, and will be glad to co-operate with you on your own lubrication problems.

NOTE: On request we will be glad to send you, without obligation, our authoritative marine lubrication treatises: "Steamships with Reciprocating Engines," and "Turbine Propelled Steamships." Write for your copies to Marine Department, Vacuum Oil Company, 61 Broadway, New York City.

GARGOYLE
Marine Oils

A grade for each type of service

Vacuum Oil Company *Specialists in the manufacture of high-grade lubricants for every class of machinery Obtainable everywhere in the world* New York, U. S. A.

The Majestic's best known Chief Engineer, Joseph P. Wolfe, shown in a 1923 advertisement.

lar speed of 23 knots had to be upped to 23½, so she would arrive in time to turn around in 24 hours and reach Southampton on schedule. Her fuel consumption cost an additional 110 tons of oil daily, increasing the expenses for the trip by $5,000.

As mentioned earlier, the White Star Line was taken out of IMM and joined to Cunard, to become Cunard White Star Line in midsummer 1934. This extraordinary reallignment was a condition of an agreement by the British government to subsidize the completion of Cunard's *Queen Mary*. Once again, two of the Ballin Big Three were sailing together, this time the *Berengaria* and the *Majestic*. In September of this year the *Majestic* was hit by a huge Atlantic wave which poured tons of water on to her upperworks. Captain Trant, her master at the time, was injured badly enough for her Staff Captain to take command. Later in the month she ran aground off Calshot, near the Bramble Bank in the Solent, but was able to refloat herself with no damage. In November of the same year, Captain Robert B. Irving, another *Majestic* master, said his ship made 24½ knots passing the *Paris* near Nantucket.

The Depression was still evident in very poor passenger lists. In May, 1935, H.P. Borer, general passenger agent for Cunard White Star, was happy to boast in a press release of a First Class list of only 266 persons. It represented a 75 percent gain over the list for the same sailing in 1934. Westbound sailings in September were always good, and on the first half of the ship's 200th round trip she carried 1,451 passengers. She encountered another severe gale that smashed three Dining Saloon ports and swept a Yorkshire terrier puppy into the sea. His name was Garbo, and he was owned by actress-impersonator Sheila Barrett. Henry Mason Day, stockbroker, had nothing to complain about, though, as he won the ship's pool four days in a row on that crossing, amassing £500 as the winnings. Upon completion of this voyage, Cunard White Star noted proudly that the *Majestic* had steamed 1,250,000 miles since her entrance into service in 1922.

November 28, 1935, was a sad day for the *Majestic*. It was on this day that word came from London that she was to be withdrawn from service after completing her February 20,

Headed for 'the dreaded 108 Berth at Southampton', the caption of this Planet News photo stated. She had just completed her 207th round trip, her last Atlantic crossing. The date of this sad photo is February 27, 1936.

'The King is Dead — Long Live the King' —
Southampton's huge dry dock being readied for the
Queen Mary, with idled Majestic at Berth 108 just
above. An Acme Photo taken March 3, 1936.

1936, eastbound crossing. Officials of the company were unwilling to speculate as to her future employment. One was quoted as confident that she would return to the New York–Southampton express service the following summer, if business conditions warranted. Another was emphatic in denying that she would follow the *Mauretania* and the *Olympic* to the boneyard. On December 9 there

were more sad stories, hinting that the *Majestic* would be broken up. It was explained that several months earlier an announcement had stated that the *Berengaria* would be withdrawn while the *Majestic* would be kept in service, but 'this plan was dropped and it was decided to keep the popular ship in service and withdraw the *Majestic* instead.' Just what the reporter who wrote this piece meant here is hard to guess, because both ships would have seemed to have been equally popular. On February 29, 1936, the Cunard White Star made it known that the *Majestic* would become a stand-by ship, at least until the *Queen Mary* came out the following May. Her last master was Captain Peter R. Vaughn. He said that he was very fond of the ship, adding that he had joined her as First Officer under Sir Bertram Hayes, and was frequently relieving captain. She was nine years younger and a full knot and a half faster than the *Berengaria*. Everyone knew her as a splendid heavy weather ship, he added.

Why the *Berengaria* was kept and the *Majestic* was laid up is hard to understand. It does seem strange that the first of Ballin's Big Three should be the last to go (it will be remembered

The Majestic, *soon to be renamed* Caledonia, *enters King George V dry dock at Southampton where her hull will be repainted before she is sent up to Scotland to serve as a Royal Navy training ship. A photo taken on December 4, 1936, by Planet News. Note how much her funnels and masts have been cut down so as she could pass under the Firth of Forth Bridge to get into the Rosyth area. (Planet News)*

laid up the *Leviathan* in the autumn of 1934). In my opinion the answer lies in the fact that the Cunard Line was the strongest of all the companies which came to own or operate the great ex-German 50,000 tonners.

But the *Majestic* was by no means finished. When the *Queen Mary* came to Southampton on March 26, 1936, for dry-docking in preparation for her speed trials, she was greeted by the idle *Majestic*, fully dressed to salute her proud successor. An aerial view taken in early May, however, showed her beginning to look a bit unkempt with only two lifeboats left on her port side. Finally, on May 17 came the word that everyone had hoped could be postponed. The *Majestic* was sold for scrap to Thomas W. Ward & Co., of Sheffield, England. But then, five months later, *Majestic* lovers were once again given news to make them smile. There was a reprieve — the magnificent ship, still with many good years of life left in her, was to be saved. She had been that the United States Lines had permanently

Caledonia *sails for Rosyth, April 16, 1937.* (Acme Photo)

acquired from the scrap yard by the British Admiralty and would serve to train orphan boys. Inquiries as to whether she might be used as a troopship were 'waived aside by Admiralty officials', one report noted. The word was that she had been traded for 24 old warships.

A month later it was revealed that she was to be renamed HMS *Caledonia* and would be ready to serve in about four months. The reconversion was to be done by John I. Thorneycroft & Co., Ltd., of Southampton, and would cost £472,000, employing 2,000 shipyard workers putting in 13 hours a day and seven days a week. In March, 1937, the job was nearly finished and the Admiralty announced that the ship would be stationed at Rosyth, Scotland. She would be the largest training ship afloat, in fact the largest ship in the Royal Navy, and she would be available as an auxiliary in an emergency. Her engines had been given a good tune up and it was stated that she would be able to develop a speed in excess of what she had maintained as a passenger vessel. A sad note—15 feet had been cut from her three beautiful funnels so she could get under the Firth of Forth Bridge and into Rosyth. She would serve 2,000 cadets.

Captain William Binks, formerly White Star master of the *Olympic*, would take her to Scotland, with Morris Evans in charge of the engine room. Much of her insides had been ripped out in the process of fitting her for cadet use, and guns had been mounted on her decks.

HMS *Caledonia* left Southampton on April 16, 1937, and she was officially commissioned on April 23. Her Old First Class Social Hall was converted into a huge gymnasium, along with the famous restaurant and palm court areas on B Deck. The cabins on C Deck were

Enough 'first class steel' was salvaged from the scrapping of the Majestic, *whose bow is shown here, to build 'between 12 and 20 cruisers', according to a British Admiralty report in 1943. The vessel was raised 'at the first attempt' and broken up in the Firth of Forth, Scotland. Some 1,800 hull openings and ports had to be sealed in the raising operation.* (Imperial War Museum)

thrown together into huge class rooms. On D and E Decks the midshipmen would swing in their hammocks. The old First Class Dining Saloon would be the messroom for the deck group, while engine room apprentices would use the old Second Class Saloon. Guns for instruction were located aft on the old Third Class deck. The topside wireless room was enlarged to accommodate up to 200 boys learning signalling. The engine rooms and swimming pool remained unchanged. The ship accommodated 1,500 youths and 500 officers and apprentices. Sir Atwell Lake, former commander of the British Admiralty's training barracks at Portsmouth, England, was appointed Commander. A night photo taken in 1939 of the HMS *Caledonia* at her berth at Rosyth showed her looking amazingly sleek, and even streamlined, with her low funnels. It appears that every light aboard must have been lit for this spectacular picture. Reflections in the quiet harbour waters were dazzling. She lay just under a huge crane similar to one that was at that very moment scrapping her sistership, the *Vaterland–Leviathan*, berthed a few hundred yards away.

HMS *Caledonia* served well, but, sadly, not for long. An Associated Press story dated September 29, 1939, led off with this strange sentence: 'There has been an outbreak of fire on the British training ship *Caledonia*. The fire was in no way due to enemy action.' The Second World War had started and everyone was on edge. The fire broke out and was subdued in the same afternoon, it was said. But at the same time the account concluded with this odd comment: 'A red glow was seen below deck and a pall of smoke hung over the ship.' The fire was more serious than initial reports indicated, and the ship actually sank in deep water because of it.

The war years passed and, on February 22, 1943, it was made known that the sunken hulk of the *Majestic*, later *Caledonia*, had been raised by divers where it had gone down. The hulk was brought inshore for scrapping. Its high quality steel was much in demand. Divers who raised the ship sealed 1,800 ports and other hull openings. She was refloated on the first attempt after pumping. It was a very, very sad ending for a magnificent liner.

POSTSCRIPT

The Ballin Big Three should have had longer, more productive lives, had they been allowed to follow the dream envisaged for them by Ballin himself. Instead of binding different peoples together through travel, the ships lived oddly truncated lives. Only the *Imperator* found herself under really able and caring management after the first great war. The *Bismarck* was afloat for 25 years but saw service for only 14 years, operating under three different ownerships during this time. The saddest and most unusual fate was left to the *Vaterland*, whose 26 years of being afloat included ten years of idleness, over three separate periods. As fate would have it she would sit unused at the very same Hoboken pier on all these occasions, first for three years before America entered the First World War, then for three more after the war, and finally for four years between 1933 and 1938. She made five voyages in mid 1934 because of public protest, but her latter life was a sad one indeed. Beginning with Hapag and followed by the US Navy, she would be controlled successively by the US Shipping Board, IMM, US Lines, the Chapman group, and finally IMM again. And yet she managed to become perhaps the most famous American liner of all time, and there are many who would insist that her company claim that she was 'the world's greatest ship' had basis in fact. Read my six volumes and then make your own decision. Both the *Berengaria* and the *Majestic* deserve more thorough books to tell their stories properly. All three beauties were extraordinary ships. Each in her own right is a candidate for the All Time Liner Hall of Fame.

Each of Ballin's Big Three can point with pride to special passenger carrying achievements on the North Atlantic. The *Leviathan* in 1927 carried 40,539—the most carried in one year by any of the three. The *Majestic* carried the most in 1924, 1926, 1928 and 1930. The *Berengaria* carried more in all the interwar years than either of her two ex-German sisters. All were winners!

INDEX

This index includes primarily ships, shipping people, shipping lines and ports.